The 1929 Depression

The 1929 Depression

Hey! That's Perry County!

Marvin Carpenter

iUniverse, Inc.
Bloomington

The 1929 Depression
Hey! That's Perry County!

iUniverse books may be ordered through booksellers or by contacting:

iUniverse
1663 Liberty Drive
Bloomington, IN 47403
www.iuniverse.com
1-800-Authors (1-800-288-4677)

ISBN: 978-1-4502-8461-5 (sc)
ISBN: 978-1-4502-8462-2 (ebk)

Printed in the United States of America

iUniverse rev. date: 08/11/2011

Marvin and Lucy Ree Carpenter

Marvin Carpenter revisiting The Old Eddy

*Marvin Carpenter and Lee Allen Travis revisiting
The Old Eddy*

Contents

A house found that is similar to one Marvin Carpenter grew up in.

Introduction

I was born in Perry County, on a one mule farm to John Palmer and Carmen Hodges Carpenter. We lived about fifteen miles from Hattiesburg, Mississippi, where we said we were "going to town" when going to Forest County. The road to town has changed since I was a kid, and now it is only a few minutes from our old place. Thanks to good transportation, the road is now shorter than it was when it was a four hour walk at a fast pace to town.

I was born on October 7, 1925, less than four years before the Great Depression. My memory is very fuzzy about when the hard times hit. Mom and Dad had a Model "T" Ford car back then for a little while before we were back on our feet to go where we needed to go. I was four years old when I was in my first car wreck, but I don't remember much about it. The steering mechanism came loose, and not being able to steer or stop the car, we came to a quick stop at the bottom of a ditch. Back then, the windshield was not safety glass. I was an easy target for a mishap being short, on the edge of my seat, and trying to see out. I went through the windshield, cutting one side of my head, on and under my chin, and under my nose. Someone came by, and to the doctor we went. The glass didn't go through my skull, so all was okay.

Alma Lee was the first child, born on November 1, 1923. She was two years older than me, and the one that I always blamed for getting me into trouble. The truth is no one held me down to make me do what things we got into. For being a girl, she did think of some neat things to do.

John Palmer Junior (J.P.) was born January 31, 1929, and the one God blessed Alma Lee and me with so we could have someone to pick on. After growing up, he was a blessing to us in many ways.

Joan was born March 14, 1940. She was too late coming for us to agitate, but we just had fun babysitting her.

I was never very smart in school. Hard times were always waiting for me when I had to study my lessons. Passing from one grade to the other was always close to a failure, but I can't seem to figure out who was to blame. The school could not teach me if I wasn't there, and my parents had only a little schooling so I didn't get a lot of teaching at home. When our winter fields produce came in, if there was a market for it and we had a chance to make a little money out of it, school had to wait. But there was another problem. The school couldn't wait and hold other people up. After all, we are a little older each day that passes. I heard Mom say at different times that we only had two books in our home, and that was the Bible and some kind of an "Esquire," something for kids. If we would have had books to read, we boys would rather have had a rat killing or something better to do than to read what someone else had written down. I guess we had enough books for us to learn from. If we really wanted to learn to read we had those two books.

School came in second place when it came down to either working in the field or being in school. Did we want to go to school and get smarter or stay in the field and survive? I know my mom and dad directed us in the right direction for doing the best thing so I never had much education, but we did survive. All wasn't bad as you can understand as you read this book.

School put a lot of pressure on me because the class would get too far along in studies while we were out so many days. One thing that was hard for me was I didn't know how to ask for help. I thought that was part of life, and tried to move on.

Summer time was not time to wear a shirt, shoes or hat. We only wore them when it was a must. There was no sunscreen to protect us from the sun, and we didn't know when we got old cancer would show up because we got too much sun in our early years. Sunscreen reminded me of using marinade on meat before putting the heat on the meat. I don't know if that is the same or not, but I guess we could have saved us a problem for our later years.

Somebody back then was concerned about our health. I don't know who it was, but they gave us a small little box with a lid that fit like a shoe shine box. We were to use it for putting a sample of our stool in and turning it into the school to have it checked for stomach worms. One family used one kid's stool for each of the kids in the family with the name of each one of the kids. The report came back for each kid to take medication to kill the worms! One kid, Bennie Lee Hensarling, who was Alma Lee's age, said the worms would not hurt the kids because she had them all her life and it didn't hurt her. I believe it, because they didn't hurt me either.

Each year we were given shots in school. That was not for me either. I felt I'd rather take a chance of dying than suffer the pain. There was no pain in shots, but our brain said there was.

Our school was large enough to have a basketball team but no other competitive sport. I liked the game, but when I finally made the first team it was when the draft board had called all the older boys in. It wasn't long until they called me into the service too.

On Christmas Eve in 1943, the mail carrier came and left a card saying to report to camp Shelby on January 19, 1944. I passed the examination and they asked which one I wanted: the Army, the Navy or the Marines. I thought of sleeping in mud, crawling among rattlesnakes, and getting hurt so I asked for the Navy and got it.

From there I was sent to Great Lakes, Illinois, for my training, and was then shipped to the Pacific Ocean where the Japanese were waiting. Hawaii was our first stop, and there I was assigned to an LCI (Landing Craft Infantry) gun boat. The LCI was a long way from being as large as the Essex, the air craft carrier ship I went over on.

We left Hawaii for a trip that was very important, an invasion of Saipan in the Marianas Islands. That was the first of five invasions in WWII for me, the last being in Okinawa, one of the Ryukyu Islands, the last battle with the Japanese.

I came home to some people who said they didn't think it was right for us to come home and take jobs they needed to feed their families. They didn't go into the service and fight. Jobs were shutting down, people were getting laid off, buildings were empty, and employment offices got crowded.

I had a job with the U.S. Engineers in Pascagoula, Mississippi, a short time before they closed down. I went to Hattiesburg to work the family farm, but that didn't work out. I went looking for work in Hattiesburg, Mississippi; Mobile, Alabama; New Orleans, Louisiana; Meridian, Mississippi; and Memphis, Tennessee. I finally found one several months later in Gulfport, Mississippi, in a sash and door mill that seemed to be a breakthrough for me in the job market.

I married a young lady, Maxine Hutson. That was the best thing that ever happened to me. Three children and sixteen years later she died of cancer. She left me with the best children from any couple: Dennis, Brenda, and Margaret. At that time I had moved to Houston, Texas, where I still live today. One and a half years later, I married a lady, Lucy Ree Clark from Beaver County, Oklahoma. She gave me a wonderful son, Derence. He seemed to be the healer of our problems when we had difficulties with each other.

I went through several jobs, and I am still working on the last job of my lifetime. At the ripe old age of eighty years old, the company has been good to let me stay and work for them. It keeps me moving this old body around for exercise, and that keeps me younger.

My oldest daughter, Brenda Sue, told me she would like for me to write down my childhood memories for my children, grandchildren, and others who will be born into the family in years to come. I gave it a shot, did my best, and hope the book will be interesting to anyone who may read it. I have had a good life, but it seems that all roads, sooner or later, will have a few rough places in it.

Marvin Carpenter

Remembering Back

Rita, the storm that came out of the Gulf of Mexico on September 23, 2005, made me think of my childhood. The storm was headed toward Houston, but it eventually turned so that the eye was to be far from us and we got a lesser part of it. I went to one of the grocery stores that next morning to get a supply of watermelons and buttermilk. I found that the stores were closed that day so I was without these things. I began to think of eating cornbread which we used to put in a glass of buttermilk and stir up. That was good then, and still good today.

Watermelon is also a good treat for us southern people now as it was back in those good old days. I miss being on the farm where I grew up. We would go out many times to eat a watermelon in the field; breaking one open by throwing it on the ground, and eating only the heart where there was no seed.

We knew just how to pick a good melon. First, we would look at the curl to see if it was dead. The curl came from the vine next to where the watermelon stem left the vine to the watermelon itself. Then, we would turn the watermelon over to look at the belly to check the color which should be turning kind of yellow by then, leaving the old white color that those things grow up with. The curl looked like a small root coming from the vine, and both the curl and color of the belly would be changing about the same time. Then, we would thump the watermelon with our finger. If it sounded with a "tink", as a plate would, it wouldn't be ready. If it sounded with a "tonk", as if it was hollow sounding, it would be time for a watermelon festival. Now, when I check a watermelon in a grocery store I miss all the good signs we used as young people in a watermelon patch. Why? Is it the way they are raised these days? Is it because of the kind of food that they are given to grow up on? Or is it me? The watermelons don't even taste as they should taste. You know, with that sweet taste those things used to have.

When I grew up, some people said a person could take colored water, put it in a jar with a grass string running from inside the jar into the stem. Then, after making a little slit to put the end of the string in, wrap it to guide the colored water inside the watermelon and change the color of the melon. I never tried it, but what about sugar water? That may make it sweet.

Buttermilk also tastes different today. What do people do when they make buttermilk for the public that gives buttermilk that twang taste? Do these people put milk in an aging tank to mature like wine in a place where air and germs can't get to it? Do they mix foreign matter with it to make it preserve? Maybe they boil or heat up to kill something in it. Oh well, that may be the reason young people don't like buttermilk today. I guess there are many of our young people that don't know how whole milk tastes today. They probably wouldn't like the stuff that tasted so good.

To prepare sweet milk for making buttermilk, we used to let it set any place in the kitchen that would be out of the way. If summertime flies were out, it would go into the kitchen cabinet we called the safe. Sometimes we would tie a piece of rag over the opening of the container (whatever it might have been). Then, we would close the screen door to the safe, and wait until the change of the milk. When the cream would rise to the top, we would skim off the cream and use part of the milk in the churn with the cream. Then, we would churn the milk by using a dasher, slosh it up and down until the cream turned into butter, take it out of the milk, and wait for eating time. We ate butter when times were hard and money was short. Now, money is big and the butter is short.

If we didn't have a churn for some reason we would put the milk in a fruit jar, and shake it up and down until the butter was ready to separate from the milk. We would get so tired we would want Mama to make one of the other kids have a turn so we could rest, but I don't remember that happening very often.

A Family with Love

As I have made notes about our family, we have laughed and joked about ourselves, each other, and sometimes at others' expense. I was grown before I knew I was very blessed to be born into the families we belonged to. As a kid, I thought everybody was like us. Taking care of each other just ran over from the good neighbors we had.

Who was our family and who were our neighbors? All our uncles and aunts were, in some way, unique in one way or another. Even though we lived in some hard days, I never heard of any of us being losers because we had loving care from family members. We were all survivors, depended on our people, and we all came through.

My generation was following a generation that would be hard to beat. Mama had two sisters and three brothers. Two of them, a boy and a girl, both died at an early age. That happened before my generation began so the two didn't have much history. Uncle Leon was the oldest of the remaining four. Being a merchant marine, he had a job most of the time, except when he would get tired of the long trips from one country to the other. Coming in from the sea, he helped the family some.

Next was my aunt Mary Lee. She made really good friends with us kids by being a good gift giver.

The last one, Mark, was born crippled. Someone had to feed him, bathe him, and stay with him most of the time. The doctors came up with the idea he may have had his neck broken during child birth because at birth the doctor had a hard time getting him to breathe. He took him by the feet with one hand and his head with the other, folding him back and forth with grandma in fear he would break Mark's back. One of the doctors said he would never live to be twenty-one, but he died at the age of seventy.

My Grandpa Hodges moved several times, depending on the work he could get. He moved from Mississippi to Alabama to West Virginia, and back to the South; back to where the jobs were.

When the families were living close to each other, they spent a lot of time together. Grandpa worked in farming, carpentry, coal mining, guard duty, ship building, and anything else he could do to keep food on the table. Daddy once told me that my grandpa could always find work if there was any work to be found.

On the Carpenter side of the family, Uncle Burkett was Daddy's oldest brother. He didn't do too well in marriage. He seemed to know when to buy food for someone else's table when he had a job, of course, and he did well in that area. He was a very good painter.

Then there was Palmer. He was my daddy. He was a good daddy to us. He spent a lot of time over at the grandparents' house with his brothers.

Next was Uncle James. He seemed good as far as keeping a job once he started working with Mr. Miller's Southern Glass and Hardware Co. He did a good job at making friends with us, too.

Next there was Uncle Oran. He worked as a section gang foreman. I remember him working for the M&O Railroad around the Pascagoula and Moss Point area. I don't know when he started working for them, but he seemed to do well at his job. When I say "seemed to do well" in depression, I am talking about survival and hard times. I don't know if these people knew the phrase "extra money."

Uncle Bernard seemed to like working on cars. I thought he must have been smart to know how to make them run. I don't remember where he worked, but farming was part of his living before the war started.

Then there was Woodroe. He spent time in Oxford, Mississippi going to college, and got into the grocery business. Mama worked with him some, and when I was in the store there was always a "hello" for me.

I don't remember much about Uncle Henry. He was killed by a train when I was pretty small. Once when Alma Lee and I were on the trail to catch the school bus, he saw us as he was going to our place to do some work for Daddy. He quickly lay on the ground and acted as if he were dead. When we saw him, Alma Lee and I walked up to him very cautiously. Alma Lee tried to wake him up, but had no luck. We walked around him wondering what to do with him. This was a new experience for us, and we just didn't understand how we fit into this puzzle. Should we go back, tell Mama, and miss the school bus or should we wait until after school? We decided to go on to school. Then, when we came home and he was gone, we would know he was still alive. If he was dead, he would still be there. When we came home, he wasn't there. We thought he woke up and moved on, and yet I wasn't too sure what happened; that is, until we saw him. That was a relief.

I wasn't around Uncle Preston much, but I remember the quiet personality he had. Once, he was doing work with Daddy when we were living above Runnelstown. He was tired and thought a nap would be good. Mama told him that the best place for a little breeze was in the living room. After he fell sound asleep, Doris and Lois Hodges, Uncle John Hodges' girls, came to visit Mama. They were teenagers, almost as old as Mama. When they saw Uncle Preston sleeping, they had a little chat and decided how funny it would be, since he had no shirt on, if he woke up with a haircut from his chest. I admit I was worried that he would be mad, and hated for the time that he would wake up. When he did wake up and found what they did, he broke out in a big laugh and stated he slept much more than he thought. Everybody joined in the laughter, and I felt very relieved.

After the war the men came home, and I had more time with him than before for a short few years. We didn't talk war, but once he did tell me that at one time when they had a prisoner, the sergeant would tell one of the men to take the prisoner to the camp and be back in three minutes. The camp was maybe three miles away so they knew what to do as they got the prisoner over behind the hill. Kill him.

After that, Alma Lee told me about the river crossing where every time a man stepped into the water he would die from a gunshot. He came back home after all that, and because of that I started having things go through my mind about what he had faced. From then on, Uncle Preston was my hero because of what he got into and he still made it home alive.

The war was to live with him until death, but when it did give him a little relief he led a good life and supported different Christian groups. His way of living made me feel ashamed of myself and my commitment.

When he knew we could use a little help with anything, he would almost beg to help if he had what it took to do the job. This was a trait that each of the Carpenters seemed to have a little bit of.

Uncle Cecil and Uncle Elton were a lot like twins. They didn't look alike, but where one was, the two usually would be together whether a ball game, the field, or at home.

Uncle Cecil seemed to be a satisfied person with a big smile and a joke to bring out a good laugh. When Uncle Cecil and Uncle Elton were left to run the homestead together or when decisions were made, they worked things out together. It looked to me like they did a good job.

One year when the beans were ready for harvest, they had Mama and us kids go over and help pick beans. When they took them to town there was no sale for them. They went home hurt, but paid Mama for our work even though they already had a loss. Mama challenged them, but they paid her saying she needed it anyway and it was a fair deal.

Uncle Cecil seemed to always think of respecting other people's feelings. A person had a reason to just naturally draw to him.

Cecil was in the World War. When he served in the jungles of Guadalcanal fighting the Japanese, he contracted Dengue fever which never went away. Once in a while, the fever would come back to let him not forget. He, too, had to live with the war and the fever in his mind for the rest of his life.

When talking about Uncle Elton, we are just about to repeat Uncle Cecil. Uncle Elton was somehow a little different in that he said just about whatever was on his mind, not thinking about what others might feel about what he thought. He wasn't like me. I hid my thoughts or deeds that kept me from standing out in front. I never heard his story about the war, but he shared with others the problems of many Americans that were in front of those enemy guns.

Wilber was the youngest of the Carpenter family. I remember he seemed to always think the other brothers liked to pick on him a little. I would feel sad about that, but I was small too. He was young enough for the three of us kids to enjoy his presence, and old enough to have some good stories.

After the war was over, and everyone was back home again I asked him about a certain letter I sent to him when he was fighting the Japanese war on Palau Islands. He couldn't remember so probably didn't get it. He was in the medic group so he saw his share of nightmares of war he would never forget. The one story he told me was there was a man using a flame thrower in a cave. When the flame thrower gave him problems, and he could not get it to work a Japanese man ran out of the cave with a fixed bayonet chasing the guy. As they ran, the Japanese man jabbed at the seat of his pants. The guy running looked as if he were trying to suck in the rear of his pants, just barely escaping the jabs of the bayonet. Wilber and his buddy watched and laughed so hard that they were down on their knees. When they got their composure and looked to see what happened, the two were gone and they never knew the climax of the story.

I thank God for each of our men and women in the generation before us, but a special thanks to the four brothers and Uncle Leon Hodges who went to war and helped to secure our freedom. Their generation lived in a time when we would never have to lock our homes or cars. It seems to have been my generation that made people lock up or lose what they worked for, and it has been getting worse ever since. Now, the guilty get more protection than the victims do from our people of the law.

I think of how lucky I am to have come from such a family as the Carpenters. I cannot think of anyone of them that would not help any of us when the need came if one of them had the help to share with us. I don't remember any of Daddy's brothers getting cross with each other. I know kids have problems, but as adults the gang was very close and enjoyed being together.

Aunt Sadie and Lavenia weren't around much once I was old enough to remember them. I only remember seeing them two times so I never got to know them. Being Carpenters, I know they were all right.

An artist's, Judy Lymer of Houston, Texas, depiction of the house that Marvin Carpenter grew up in.

That Was My Mama

I was born on October 7, 1925, in Perry County, Mississippi, only a short time before the Great Depression in which happened in 1929. This was a time when economically the whole world must have been hit very hard. Mama and Daddy were married long enough that they had bought forty acres of land from his mother and daddy, built the home we lived in, had three children and one miscarriage. There wasn't much money, but we had the necessities of life, as we knew them, and a lot of tough love. I heard Mama tell the story about the same year the depression swallowed us up, there was also a bad drought that gave us a very hard stomach punch.

As the field and garden were trying so hard to produce something for families to eat, Mama and Daddy prayed for God to supply our needs and would then set out to harvest whatever they could find to eat for the day. This happened every day. They would always find something produced just enough for that day.

The depression must have been bad for everyone, but worse on people trying to do their best for their kids. They were raising kids, and those not owning their homes but renting, must have had it really bad.

Mama said she had two babies at once, Alma Lee and me, which needed to be rocked to sleep at the same time. Alma Lee was two years older than I was and we must have been a problem. She improvised a way she was able to do just that without help. She had a kid's wagon and a rocking chair, but needed two laps to put two babies to sleep. After thinking the thing over, she tied the wagon to the rocking chair. As the chair rocked to and fro the wagon also rolled to and fro, putting both babies into a restful sleep.

The third baby came in 1929, the same year as the depression. Raising us three kids during that time must have been worse than potty training a duck.

We did without a lot of things, but there was one thing we had plenty of and that was a mother's love. When we got hurt, she was the one that kissed the hurt away. When we needed a hug, she was the one that showed up for the chore.

There was a time we needed hats in the heat and bright sunlight, but no money. She made each of us kids a bonnet. Mama was a very talented person and sewing was no problem to her. We thought they looked so good, and they were cool too. Those things were well used.

Once we had aprons, also, but we didn't really need those. It was more of a gift than a need, but we thought they were all right. It was a lot of fun to do what grownups do. There were many people making garments for their families, but aprons and bonnets? Mama didn't seem to mind doing the sewing of our clothes, but she liked sharp scissors. When J.P. and I used her scissors on rubber for sling shots, she seem to always know we had been around.

We seemed to be the only two that would take the edge off her scissors. We heard the news, anyway.

There isn't much we can say about our mother without describing everyone's mother who was a good one. It seems our mother was different though. I think we kids came first with my mama. When Daddy was working away from home he was living a life that many stories could be told about while anyone's mama was at home wiping everything on her kids, from their nose to their tail and then some. I think, in general, mamas have more endurance than daddies when it comes to kids. A man holds a baby in his arms when it needs attention until he gets tired. Our mama would hold us until she got tired and then hold us a little longer, a little longer, and a little longer. A daddy would put a child down three times before a mama would dump her child. Maybe she was trying to raise us up to be like people she could put up with in her later life.

I said before we got two pair of overalls and a pair of shoes at school starting time. One year when winter came on and it was time to start wearing shoes, my feet had sores all over them. Mama said they would stay that way all winter because of wading in the cow lot everyday or as long as the rain kept the lot wet. Mama let me stay out of the lot as much as she could, but the chores had to be done so it was an everyday thing for me to wade in the lot both morning and evening. When I was through I would wash my feet in a pan of warm water and let Mama put medicine on them. Talk about a pan of water; the pan was our bathtub! That was a long winter.

Mama always did her best to take care of her kids. If we got hurt, she kissed the pain away or whatever it took to make us feel good. If our skin got too tight and we needed loosening up, she looked for a good switch to make us feel bad.

Mama always seemed to worry about us boys getting together with loose women and a strong drink, and she raised us to keep a long distance from both. I wondered why she was so strict. Me being just a kid, I couldn't see why she was so afraid. I thought we were among the best, but after years piling up on us we did learn to sneak around a little with the corn liquor, peanuts, cane, and watermelons and smoking things like grape leaves and such. We had people in the family that used the strong drink. We could see from them what alcohol could do when buried deep into the body, and how it still went all the way to the head and knocked out the transformer to the brain. We had two in the Carpenter bunch and two from the Hodges men that were good teachers that we could learn from. The way some of us played around with some of it, I guess there could have been a danger if we had let it. I think we had enough fear of our mama to keep us fairly safe until we got old enough to use what little sense we had.

Mama told of a time when she went to the Carpenters' home. Wilber was the youngest of Daddy's brothers, and their home was like ours; hedged all the way across the front yard. Wilber had made some home brew and stuck it into the hedge to hide it from the other boys. Some person or persons found it, and only the culprit and God knows where it went. Wilber was mad. He searched for his possession, cried, and wanted to know who got his home brew. That got Mama's attention, but it really wasn't any of her business and she couldn't do anything about it. I think that made her hope very strongly that we kids wouldn't be into making and indulging in the brew.

I don't know if he found out who did what with his stuff. Of course, he never became an alcoholic or such so he turned out okay. He did turn out to be a hunter much of his time. I wonder if that was caused by him looking for his home brew so long when he was a kid.

The days were hard on Mama when we kids were growing up. I feel I know how Mama felt with life and the economy being very bad: worried about life's needs and kids that called on her day and night, even when we could have been okay, while she was trying to collect her thoughts on what she and Daddy could do to change an ugly situation into a very loving and caring thing with the family they had. Time has changes in it, and it must have seemed to her like those hard days had no end until death was to come. Whether Daddy was home with her or if he was away looking for work, she would dig into the dirt in the field trying to get food to come out of it so she could feed us. In her spare time she would be patching clothes or any other things that needed to be done. The ground needed to be fertilized, but it was like us, doing without also. She would go into the woods and rake away the fresh leaves or straw to get that which was already starting to decompose. I think she called it mulch. She would put it in a grain sack, throw it over her shoulder, and go to the field to feed the soil. That was a very slow and tiring chore. There was not enough to do the entire field that way, but our garden had some priority over the rest of the field. At least some of the dirt had help. We kids did very little to help Mama, but what we did made us feel like we were a lot of help. The field got most of the manure from the cow lot, but the garden got the mixture of both.

Daddy would borrow money from the bank sometimes to raise a crop, but there were other times he and Mama couldn't see how they could pay it back if they borrowed the money. Daddy borrowed two hundred dollars from Uncle Oren Carpenter, his brother. He couldn't catch up on bills to pay it back until the depression was over and the war caused the economy to bring jobs back so we could all have a little money in our pockets. I believe Uncle Oren felt good to see his money come back.

Mama had Alma Lee and me to make things harder for her. We always fussed at each other and demanded her attention. She probably thought it would be nice to send the two of us ahead to the Promised Land before they left themselves.

J.P. came along the same year the depression hit us. He had cases of pneumonia plus a bad foot that didn't grow right which caused him very much pain. I still think she had a lot less trouble with him than us older kids. Joan wasn't there yet for a few more years. When she did come along I think she was what Mama really needed. It seemed that the two of them were able to have more time together because of the changing times, and they seemed to have more joy with each other; more so than the rest of us. She didn't give Mama the kind of treatment that us older kids did, and life got somewhat easier after the war started. The jobs opened up which gave Mama a chance to go to Pascagoula. She got a job working for Broomfield's Clothing Store out of the hot sun. She had burned out three times over the years from the hot sun. Back then, people said when a person got over heated like that it took about three years to overcome it. That would cost her nine years of trouble.

There were times it seemed worse for me to make Mama happy. I would try so hard to stay away from bugging her about anything and try to do extra little things to keep from upsetting her, yet it seemed to be a losing battle. It looked as if she was looking for good reason to reprimand me. I am sure the other two kids felt the same way, but I only remember about me. Daddy was talking to me about something. I don't know what it was about, but I told him of my feelings that I couldn't make Mama happy regardless of what I did.

He said, "Well, you know what is making her that way, don't you?"

I said, "No sir, I don't."

He said, "Ah, come on now. You do know why she is that way, don't you?"

"No sir, I don't know. I try hard to please her, and I can't do anything that will help."

"Ah, come on!"

I said I still did not know. He seemed kind of disappointed with me. "She is going to have a baby!"

I answered with, "Well, she told Alma Lee and me that she was never going to have another baby because it was hard on her having to take care of us rowdy kids and putting up with us!"

He said, "Well, regardless of what she said, she is going to have one."

I knew that at my age and my experience I ought to know all about the what's and how's of barn yard multiplication, but my Mama said . . .

Oh well, what's next now? Mama said she would never have another kid to bug her, and what she said would be the gospel. She was big enough to back up what she said, too. Now, am I supposed to want to put up with an angry woman and her ways when I had nothing to do with her problem? Oh well, the problem became a blessing to all of us and was worth it all. She was like new grass in the spring.

Remembering Mama and her cooking, sometimes I wonder if it would taste the same now or if we liked it for some other reason. Turtle meat was one of the delicacies that we enjoyed. Back then, people said the turtle has seven different flavors in their meat. I have often wondered how people would distinguish seven different tastes in one animal, although I know some meat has different tastes. What an animal eats probably changes the tastes, but all of it producing different tastes in one animal? Maybe they were talking about different parts having different tastes; like the brain doesn't taste like chitterlings and so on.

Then there were duck eggs Mama would cook for us when they were available. The duck's eggs tasted kind of strong. Mama said she believed that was because the duck ate at the branch that ran along beside the house. There was plenty of crayfish, small fish, tad poles and other critters that live in the slough, branch, lake or wherever there was mostly standing water. Ducks seem to like feeding in still water. I think maybe we liked them because the duck eggs were so much larger than hen eggs. We didn't always have ducks either.

We didn't always have turtle eggs either, but May and June were good months to visit Tallahala River to hunt the eggs. Mama knew how to cook them, too. Maybe we liked them because they were so much smaller than hen eggs. Now that my childhood has disappeared, I have no Mama to cook the good stuff. With me being an old man, I wonder how to cook as she did. I don't know any more about how to cook turtle eggs than I know how a snake drinks water.

Now, how did Mama cook those fish-eels? I think she fried them like she fried the fish. In today's world, most people I suppose throw those goodies away, but we didn't waste very much food. Now, when we catch an eel we don't want to get our hands dirty and they are very slimy. The way we got a grip on them was get a handful of sand. That made it much easier to hold them to get them off the hook. If we had problems holding them after we got home to clean them, we had a rag and could hold on pretty good.

Then were the days of popcorn. I could always feel the mother's love when we had popcorn. Mama seemed to enjoy seeing us kids enjoying life and popcorn.

Then there was pull candy. I still don't know how to mix and make the stuff, but I knew how to treat it when time came to pull, stretch and roll that treat from heaven! The best part of making the candy was our Mama would never allow us to handle our food at the table, except biscuits; but with pull candy, we were turned loose. It was so nice to do the things we really weren't supposed to do and get by with it being ready, willing and able! Eating the stuff wasn't so bad either.

I had ear aches very often, and there were times they broke open and let a little blood ooze out. There were not many things that helped to ease the pain as we have now. There were different remedies, but they either didn't work or didn't sound good. One of the remedies was to take Betsy bug grubs, then mash them up, and put that in the sore ear. Then the Betsy bug itself would have a drop of oil in the hinge part of its body that you could take after breaking it open and put it in the troubled ear.

Mama said she didn't believe that was the answer. For one reason, she didn't believe the Betsy bugs had that oil in them. I thought of that, but wouldn't say anything because I didn't know how to say what I was thinking. When I was alone and had a chance, I took one, broke it down, and found no oil. I wondered if I looked in the wrong place for that oil.

Fishing was one of the things that kept food on the table. Fishing was for summer sport and summer food. Hunting was for winter sport and winter food. Mama or Daddy never sent us out to do either one of these. It was just what we liked to do. We felt good when we could bring meat home, clean it, salt it down and put it in the safe by the stove for a meal later.

One day J.P. went to the Tallahala River and put out some lines. When he went back and ran them, he found he had picked the right day, the right weather, and the right place. He pulled the lines out and had six catfish to take home. Each one of them weighed around two pounds each which to us would be a big fish. When he came out of the woods and got to the Pearce home at the end of the road to the highway nineteen, Mrs. Pearce was out in the yard. They spoke and Mrs. Pearce bragged on him for catching the fish. J.P. offered to give her a couple of them. After all, the worms we dug up were out of their lot, and the fences we crawled over and through were theirs. J.P. felt comfortable giving the fish to her, and she accepted them with a smile which would have made anyone happy to see. Both were happy and on to the house he went. The mistake he made was telling Mama what he did. She started fussing at him for giving the fish away. I don't think Mama ever found out all his business after that. J.P. was thinking payback time while Mama was thinking food on the table. Back then, food wasn't always plentiful, but as some used to say, "A blind hog will find an acorn someway." I guess the moral to this story is to never share your story with anyone if the story sounds a little fishy.

That Was My Daddy

My daddy was a good man, but not perfect just like the rest of us. He had some faults, but he had good qualities also. I will try to describe his actions, how he joked and how he thought. I believe he was much like we imagine when we think of older men of Mississippi in years past. I hope people will think as much of me one day, as the people in the past thought of him. He was a man who seemed to enjoy helping other people, to the extent of ignoring family time when it may have been important to someone else to tend to family, in order to help one of his neighbors. I believe there was something inside of him that sometime controlled his mind. I had heard of Grandma Carpenter having too many children to be fair, with having time to share with each of them one on one as much as she needed to for them to all feel loved as children should. On the other hand, our culture was so different than today. Now our kids sometimes grow up without enough work to do and get their minds working the wrong thoughts. With mothers and fathers both having to work out of the home place and everyone else in the family having too much idle time on their hands, I think there is something that pushes us from time to time in directions we don't really want to go. I have heard that when slaves were freed, people had more children born in the family to take the place of slaves in the fields and elsewhere.

I believe when a daddy takes a boy or girl out for fun like to a ball game, a movie, to the beach or anyplace, the child will feel so important to be with and share in the fun with "my daddy". The child will stand tall and proud to be really somebody in the eyes of a good daddy.

When a man takes two or more children out for the same fun thing, the children have more in common with their own age group and start having fun with each other more than with Daddy now. Daddy is more of a pleasing guide to the children instead of the "pal daddy" that would otherwise exist with the one child. The more children, the more of a counselor figure Daddy becomes. To me, the one-on-one time will not always be best, but there is a time for it, even if there is more than one child in the family. We can all have a turn to be important with Daddy, but with a large family? My daddy came from a family of thirteen children.

When Maxine and I started raising children, a co-worker at Folgers Coffee Co. told me about a neighbor of his who had two boys, a yard full of holes, and the grass was a mess. Someone stopped by his house, and the two men started talking. The visitor asked the father of the boys why he had not stopped the boys from messing the yard up with holes all in it. The place was a mess. The father said, "I am raising boys, not grass." I thought that was my daddy. He didn't talk it, he did it. J.P. and I had a lot of holes in our yard. No one said, "No."

Daddy was more than a daddy. He was a provider in a troubled time. When our nation is in trouble it seems that the whole world is hurting. Daddy let Mama do the dirty work of raising kids and using the rod or switch on us. I don't remember him whipping us very often.

We seemed to have enough food, which I understand was one of the biggest depression problems. Sometimes it might have been only buttermilk and cornbread, or bread and turnips, or things like that to eat. We did raise our corn so we had corn meal for bread. Our chickens only needed a little food to keep them from running off someplace in the summer time. In the winter we fed them corn that we raised. One of my friends told me his family had three meals a day. At breakfast they had oatmeal, at noon corn meal, and at night no meal. I thought he must have remembered how the depression was.

Many people had to leave their homeland to look for any kind of work. My daddy was one of the many that left his family to try finding work. When he heard of a job, he answered its calling.

Mama moved to Pascagoula for a while to be with Daddy. He moved there after finding a job with the U.S. Engineer in a dredge boat repair and supply yard. They had interesting neighbors there. In fact, Pascagoula was more of an active place as far as getting out and mixing with other people than in those woods around Runnelstown. Those people stayed on the move and were carefree. No cows to milk at the end of the day, no wood to take into the house, no hogs to slop, and no mule or chickens to take care of. When eight hours of work in a day was over, time was taken for visiting, fishing or whatever a loose man wanted to do. With no T.V., no radio, and no telephone it was a much different world and culture than we have today.

One day, a neighbor asked Daddy if he could take him to town so he could take care of some banking business. Daddy was freed up, so he told him yes. He could take the neighbor. No problem. The wife came out so she could go and not be left alone at the house, just bored, sitting around with no one else around and nothing to do.

They had about two miles to go from Bayou Casotte to Pascagoula, and were talking about the day at work or whatever men talk about on the way to the bank. After getting to the bank, Daddy found a place to park and the neighbor, Mr. Reid, got out of the vehicle and went on in. Mrs. Reid and Daddy had that entire truck seat to themselves. Now, the Reids lived across the old dirt street from Mama and Daddy so they saw each other almost daily and were no stranger to each other.

Daddy and Mrs. Reid sat there for a while, and I can almost see them getting quieter and quieter. Then she spoke up and said, "Let's go for a ride."

Daddy said, "We better wait because Reid may come out and would want to know where we are."

She said, "Oh, we have plenty of time."

"We don't know how long he will be in there, and he is expecting for us to be here so we are going to wait."

By now, Daddy is starting to sweat.

Mrs. Reid says, "There is a long line in there, and he is going to be in there for a long time."

"I don't see how you know because you haven't been inside and seen the line."

"That line is always long, and we have plenty of time to spend together without him."

Daddy was going to be a good neighbor to Mr. Reid, not to her, so he wouldn't move. She must have had him in a good sweat, because he always kept some distance between himself and the loose women. He never felt the same about his "across the street" friends again after that scare. He saw her as a predator, and he was the prey. I didn't know he was so afraid of women, and he didn't have a "come unto me" look, but that's my daddy.

Another time, Daddy was having trouble with his back. He needed to work, but he didn't need to hurt while he worked. After all, he was the daddy around the house and needed to be the provider for his family. He had Mama to rub his back with liniment or whatever they could think of that may help his back. He finally gave up and went to see a chiropractor. He paid for fourteen treatments to try and get his back in working condition again. He made his regular trips in hopes all would work out, and it did seem to work. It seemed to me he made progress with each appointment until he was at the doctor's office for his ninth treatment. He was on the table with his clothes off while the doctor was doing his workout. Then the nurse called out that someone wanted to see him for a moment. The doctor went off while my daddy lay there waiting for the doctor's return when the door opened up. Here came a woman nurse walking in and through his present surroundings while he is laid out for the doctor's observation and rubdown, which usually is private.

Daddy was watching her as she walked through at a normal pace and acted as if she was on a regular routine, as was part of her job. He watched her, but I don't know if she looked at him or what she saw. Daddy waited until she went on through to wherever it was that she was going. Then, he got up, put on his clothes, not waiting for any doctor, and walked out to never return. As far as I know he never saw that man or woman again. The doctor may, after all these years, be waiting for him to come back and get his money's worth for the service owed to him. My daddy wasn't only afraid of women, but he had morals too. Good ones at that. I wonder what my mama would have done if she had walked in on the scene with Daddy without clothes on, lying on the table, and a woman in the room as if she was looking for something. That's my daddy!

Uncle Oren Carpenter lived near Moss Point, in one of the railroad homes near the tracks. He was a foreman of the railroad track repair crew. We didn't always have a good way of transportation, but we did go visit them on a few occasions. It seemed so good to go into a different world once in a while. We enjoyed our visits when we went.

Uncle Oren and Aunt Georgia Lee treated us very well. They were living in one of three houses that were close to a turn bridge that crosses the Escatawpa River. That was such a neat thing! To know they really turned that bridge so the boats could go through when it was open, and the train could cross the river when it was closed. It stayed open most of the time for the boats. The train had a schedule to meet, but the boats didn't. They came through most any time.

There were some of those large southern oak trees that had limbs reaching down toward the ground. It was as if they had arthritis in them and just couldn't hold those large things up, and kind of relaxed them. I don't think anyone ever lived long enough to know how old those things were. They were homes for a lot of wildlife like rodents, birds and such. The marsh was by the river which was close by. The old crab hole was there with a boat for the boys to enjoy fishing and watching out for an alligator that came by on an occasion who checked to see if it was safe with the boys at home, not in his home. We enjoyed the hole. When we got tired of fishing, we could sit on the track and watch the boats go by, running up and down the river. The first marsh rat I had ever seen was in the area around the marsh grass that grew about head high. I think that it is limited to what can live in that stuff. The marsh rat looked like it was almost as large as a grown opossum in the eyes of a boy.

A good place to catch crabs is either in the crab hole, the river, or in the Gulf of Mexico, which is only a short drive. We could drive there to pick up shells. Kids there had a lot of loose time, not having fields or stock to care for. I don't remember the season, but sometime in the year the Fiddler crabs would fill the roads near the Carpenters' home. It was sad that people had to run over them, but they wouldn't get out of the way. They made a feast for the ants, crows or whatever would eat them. I don't know why they would travel with such a crowd. Bob Bradley, my son-in-law, said it has something to do with the mating season and thinks they were on their way to fresh water to give birth to their young. I think he is right because that is what the salmon do up north. They came out of the ocean and moved up those rivers where the streams had fresh water and gravel bottoms. Otherwise, they don't lay eggs.

On one of our trips, we four boys showed up and there was some loud talking as if the fellows didn't like each other. J.E. and Junior knew these guys. In fact, they were neighbors, and it sounded like there was bad blood between the boys. After a consultation, they began throwing sticks and stuff at each other, but not at J.P. and me. One of our cousins, I don't know now which one, started throwing dirt, and it went into one of the other boys' eyes. They both left running. We went on about our business for a while, and it got time to go back to their house. Uncle Oren and Daddy were waiting for us. The neighbors to J.E. and Junior went home and told their daddy. The daddy had gone over to report to Uncle Oren what the boys had done to his son. He was quick about it, and we were kind of stunned. We didn't realize the boy could go home, tell the story about the dirt in his eyes to his daddy, his daddy would talk to Uncle Oren, get it off his chest and leave all before we got there.

Uncle Oren confronted the boys about the incident and wanted to know what their story was. As they were telling Uncle Oren, he laid down the law not to lie to him about it. They were giving him some back talk to make him understand they didn't start it. As they were arguing back and forth, Daddy spoke up and told me to speak up and tell what happened "because he won't lie." My daddy meant well to put me up on a pedestal, but I sure didn't want to be engaged into an argument that belonged to someone else. Uncle Oren told me to tell him the story. I felt as though I was standing in a court room facing the judge and jury. Oh, I hated to say anything. Now, looking back, I think my daddy was using psychic powers on me by saying that he knew I wouldn't let him down. I felt that Junior and J.E. did what the other kids forced them to do. Will they believe me when I tell the truth? I did the best I could to tell it as I saw it, and none of us got in trouble. I felt that I had Daddy's trust in me.

Daddy was telling me about a lightning storm coming up. He ran to the house and got away from the rain and lightning because he didn't like all that popping and cracking in the atmosphere. He felt safer on the inside of the house. I asked him, "Daddy, you are a Christian. Are you afraid to die?" Daddy was a good man and a deacon at Runnelstown Baptist Church, trying to raise us kids to be a good up right people. He said, "Well, I don't like being out in the storm like I am tempting the lightning to strike me, but if it comes inside the house and gets me, that would be okay."

Joan said they had a lightning storm when she was a girl and remembers following Daddy from the front of the house to the back, watching the weather and the lightning. She asked him if he was afraid, and he said, "What should I be afraid of?" She knew he was hiding something from her to keep her from being afraid. I think he was trying to give her help to be brave when he needed someone to help him overcome the fear himself. That was my daddy.

One time Daddy had a little time on his hands. It was late afternoon and getting close to evening time, when the heat of the day started fading away and the mosquitoes feeling supper time coming on. It was a time to be tired and glad the day was about to wind down. Daddy was in the front yard, feeling good with us kids around. He went over to the steps that led upon the front porch where we had spent many hours of many days watching the sun going down in the west. Back then, that was the closest thing to television that we had. It was a good time to visit to share stories of the day or questions of life to ask about or just pick at each other for laughs. That really was a good way to finish up the day and get prepared for a good night's sleep, as soon as supper was devoured, the dishes washed and the body was cleaned with a wash pan full of water, a little soap plus working up energy. Rags were made from ragged clothes or bed sheets that served its time in bed which then worked its way up from giving sleep to a tired mosquito bitten body to giving it a bath in preparation for a good night's rest.

When he sat down, we kids went over and sat down with him feeling comfortable being in the presence of our daddy, our protector, our provider. Alma Lee sat close enough to him that she was leaning over with her elbow resting on his leg, and her chin was resting in her hand. I had too many problems with ear aches until I couldn't hear very well. Daddy started whispering my name and would get louder and louder until I would jerk my head around, finally hearing, and answer as my name was called. Then Daddy and Alma Lee would start laughing. This went on with the two of them after a few rounds before changing thoughts of something else. We were all having fun as a good memory. I have shared that with people now that times have changed all of us, and they would say something like, "That was awful having your daddy to do you that way, being hard of hearing!" My response was and still is, "What could they do to heal my ears instead of having fun with me?" We all were having fun and it still is another good memory of my daddy. Most of us like to not be ignored but attentions paid to us. Now that was my daddy.

Daddy was working down in what we called the "Buck Creek Flats" on a new portion of road, and somehow he broke the hide on one of his fingers. He went to one of the homes of people he knew, and the lady told him to come on in. She got medication and a rag, started cleaning him up, and got the blood and dirt out and the medication in. She got it all wrapped up and asked if it seemed to be okay. Daddy thought she did a fine job. The lady asked, "Since we have that taken care of, is there anything else I can take care of now?" As Daddy said, "Naw," he was scratching for the door. She was looking for business, and he was not a business man. That was my daddy!

Daddy brought home a dog that gave us a chance to do more rabbit hunting and bring in some meat. He showed off the dog and watched it run around to all of us, so happy, wagging its tail and just couldn't be still. Maybe the dog didn't know yet that this was home now, and the home he knew didn't exist anymore so there was no turning back. Who knows what a dog is thinking? It may be the dog wanted a different diet than just a little corn bread and turnip greens and go where the meat was. Who can tell? Daddy told me the dog was mine, to take care of it and let it help me hunt and bring in some meat. Any place us boys were, the dog was part of the clan whether it was in the woods, at the lake or river, in the field or around the barnyard. That dog was almost like family. J.P. and I would hunt with him. When we got a rabbit or squirrel, we would take it home and the dog would be so happy, walking with us and our kill as if the dog was a proud part of the winning of the game. He was hoping we would hurry home and divide the critter with him, as if that was going to be like an ice cream party. Now it just wasn't going to be like that. This is what he could expect; we boys would pull out our knife and start with the skin, then the stomach parts, the head, then the feet. Sorry, we got the meat; the dog gets what is left. The head, feet, skin and inner parts as if the dog didn't do much to help, but without the dog there would be no supper. It took a long time before that registered with me. After all, the dog could wait until we got it cooked and ate, then after that the dog could have the cooked bones. What is better than that? Our fun with that dog came to an end later; Daddy gave him away to someone else. No explanation. The dog was to give up our home and hope his next home would be better. I didn't know how it would be better than what he had. After all, he owned two boys to run with, a comfortable place to lie under the house where it was cool in the summer, and in the winter it was warm by the fire place chimney base at the end of the house.

I was too young to realize it wasn't just my dog, but a family dog that the family got some good out of him. I didn't know any reason to lose my pet. Someone should have explained something to me. I think I have made much worse mistakes with my kids after I became a father, so I still realize my daddy was a good daddy after all. He was still my daddy. Oh! By the way, even though a dog seems so happy to be with its master, and as they feel people are looking at them like they are happy to be in the dog's presence, but what about the dog in his quiet time just lying around thinking as their minds wonder around. Do dogs still miss its mother, sisters and brothers?

Sometimes it is hard to be someone when you feel like you are no one, and all the others are better at everything than you are, and you want so badly to be accepted in anything. Even a rabbit is good for one meal, but me? I kind of liked being alone. I didn't need too many people to spend time with. Every time I seemed to reach, there would be something come along and set me back. I must know how Moses felt when he could look out, see the

Promised Land, and be told by God he shall never enter in it after all those forty years of trying so hard to get there. It seemed to be a vapor. No one wants to chase a vapor, but we all have our own to chase sometimes, I guess, and at the time I had mine.

We had been invited to eat a noon time meal with the Birch family who lived at Runnelstown on the Richton Road. When leaving Runnelstown toward Richton, they lived in a house just before starting up a hill where the Miller home was. We had never eaten at their house, even though they were a part of the community and used the same church, same school, the same grocery store and had the same friends. We really didn't have bad people as we think of them today. Maybe we all slipped a little sometimes, but not these people and they were friends with everybody. Alma Lee and I didn't know how to act at a dinner table. We were nervous, as if all eyes were going to be on us, and not like our family who tried to ignore us. The ladies had their hellos out of the way, and Polly was just about through getting the meal together. The women got together on what was needed to do to get food on the table and who did what. The two men caught up on any new or old news they could think of (and back then they called it gossip if it had been the women talking) while the ladies did what ladies do and we kids just sat around waiting for food. After all, that was why we were there, not standing or sitting around and talking. When all were as ready for us as we were ready for it, we were all seated round the table. We kids were treated as if we were King George VIII, as we were seated and our plates were filled with a big fat steak with all that other stuff that needed to be company with that big old piece of meat.

The prayer was said, but asking the Lord to help me get my meat cut wasn't in the prayer. It should have been mentioned to God because I was going to be as proper as I could be. When I put my fork and knife into that meat, and my knife cut down across that thing, it seemed to come alive, slid out of my plate, and just jumped right on the floor between Mama and me. I felt I wanted to hide from the rest of the clan, but kids don't do that often enough to be trained what to do or say. Neither are the daddies well trained what to say after that kind of show the son performed at the table.

Daddy said, "Well, Son!"

Steak in those days didn't just lie around on anybody's table all the time. As I looked down on that meat, I wished it would jump back up, but it didn't. I didn't know what to do. Mama and Polly, both at the same time, jumped up to get that poor thing, and then argued about which would trade meat with me. Polly won that time as she wiped the dirt off and placed it on her plate. Mama helped me by cutting the new meat up for me as I felt so bad. The group around the table was so good to me, having their own excuse for the ordeal with stories of their own. For some reason or other, I was never invited to that home for another dinner show. When Daddy said, "Well, son", I was already at the bottom of distress and self-conscious so I couldn't have been any worse, but I never got any "I'm sorry" from Daddy. I am and always have been one that could never say I'm sorry. The words just wouldn't come out of my mouth. So maybe I know why and who I got it from. He was still my daddy.

When summertime came, the fields had been planted, seeds germinated well in good soil, and plants had been well taken care of. If the moisture was good for that time of year and there was enough money for fertilizer, the plants would always grow good produce on somewhat soil. That was with a good clay foundation. We had a time for canning whatever developed full grown and ripe. That was a family activity. What I liked most about canning was the harvest part of it. We kids and the grass grew up together and neither the grass nor we kids got in each other's way most of the time. After lay by time, which was the time we would turn loose a crop from our labor, then it was time to withdraw, worry, wonder and wait until it gave us payback by producing food for our work.

Sometimes we let some of our bounty like peas, okra, string beans, butter beans, melons and such dry. They stayed good unless bugs, rats or something else desired to feed on it before we had time to either eat or plant it. It was hard for anything to get into it when we used glass jars or syrup cans some of the times.

I remember one such day, when Daddy and I were shelling peas. Mama said something about us shelling so many peas so fast, and we had been doing our best.

Daddy spoke up and said in a voice that made me think he was aggravated with me, "He is the one that is shelling the most of these. I can't keep up with him!"

Mama saw I was beginning to cry and said, "Daddy, you shouldn't talk like that about him! He thinks you're mad!"

Daddy said, "Well, I was just picking at him. I didn't mean to make him cry!"

I did let Daddy shell peas with me again. After all, he was my daddy.

Another time we were all getting ready for bed. Daddy disappeared for a few minutes, came back in the room where we were, and said something to get our attention. When I looked, there was my daddy, wearing one of my mama's gowns. I was so shocked and didn't realize what was going on. Do I have two mamas? Or what do I have? I began to cry and didn't understand why Daddy left the room. Mama went over to me and gave me a hug while both her and Daddy were laughing and enjoying every bit of it! I was still my Mama's crybaby, he was still my Daddy, and I never saw that happen again!

Sweet potatoes were one of our regulars in the field. On one of our work days we were fighting tall grass in the potato rows, and I was a little naughty. It wasn't what I was doing that I remember, but the payback is what sticks in my mind. Daddy was trying to get my mind on the work that we had to go out and take care of. When he gave up on words, he looked for something to use on me that would make an impression on me. The only thing that was close by was the potato vines. Most any other time there would be persimmon bushes close by, but maybe God liked me a little about then. Daddy sized up a potato vine, tried it out for his own satisfaction, and came up to me mind you, not waiting on me to go to him. Short legged overalls must have looked good to him because it was my legs that stopped the swing of that potato vine. I have heard of someone being beat black and blue most of my life. When he got happy and let me overcome my wilted down body, I looked down and saw those blue marks on those skinny little legs. Oh! I just couldn't wait to show Alma Lee what my daddy did to me, but she was a little smart for me. I didn't know the blue would come off the vine and be on my fingers or legs. When a sweet potato vine grows with that blue coloring, there is a little powder that will stay on someone's hands when they make contact with it, but it doesn't stay on as a dye. It washes off quite easily.

Alma Lee saw what I was talking about when I was trying to convince her how black and blue my Daddy whipped me, and didn't even feel sorry about any of it. That was worse than the whipping Daddy did on me, and I thought I got that for nothing. Just wait until Alma Lee got herself a whipping! I'm not going to feel sorry for her either.

Daddy and Horace Shoemake joined together once and bought the lot in front and across Highway 42 from the Dennis' store in Runnelstown. They decided to sell it. His share was a few cases of Coca-Cola, and that looked so good to us kids. We liked anything that was sweet, and we only got one of those glass bottles when someone wanted to see some happy children because, after all, they cost a nickel each. The company would give one or two cents if they got the bottle back so they could use them again.

I wouldn't mind having that lot for myself now. I wonder what it would cost. I still remember the large oak tree that stood next to the highway. People would park under it for the shade while they went into the store.

Around the Barnyard

We had a lot of fun around the barnyard. A lot of stories could have leaked out from our knowledge, and there aren't many of us left. Stories have gone into eternity with the dead. We need J.P. to open up with his stories! I don't know why he can remember so much more than I can, and I am older than he is. I think one thing that keeps us from remembering more is because we accept what comes along, and everything we do is a part of our culture and we have no reason to hold it in our minds.

One day, for some reason, J.P and I weren't going to be able to feed the cows. I really don't remember what Mama wanted the cows fed with. Alma Lee had never had to work with the cows, so she could easily be frightened by them, but it was a job that needed to be done. We had a young cow that J.P. and I had played with since her birth, and we had taught her a game. We taught her to butt us when we bowed down and stuck our tail ends up toward her. When she got pretty good, we would wait for her to start running, and then we would stand up before she got to us. Well, Alma Lee didn't want to go near the cows, but Mama told her to do it anyway because the cows would not bother her. With great caution, she eased the gate open, went in and made it almost to the crib when the cows, thinking she was going to feed them, started running after her. As fast as she was running she must have been air born part of the way before she got to the door, opened it, climbed in and started screaming and crying, calling Mama. Now, Mama came out really mad. She looked around for a stick, either to whip Alma Lee or the cows, but I think she was planning to initiate Alma Lee into the real world. She spotted a stick, went over to pick it up, and as she bent over to pick it up, the young cow saw her and the race was on! Mama got up and was okay, so was the cow. Mama let us know that if we wanted to enter Hades a little early, just play the game with that cow one more time. I guess you are wondering if we did. Well, J.P. and I are still here but Mama is gone, Alma Lee is gone and the cow is gone. The reason J.P. and I are still here is because we believed Mama. We did enjoy playing with the cows and sometimes gave them a hug. I liked to feel of the skin when I hugged, but I have never heard of a cow shaving.

When we had a bull born at our house, we would wait until he got large enough for us to ride without him getting hurt, not thinking he thought nothing about us getting hurt. We had one that was different than the others. He had messed with us so much, I guess, he also got smart. We would catch him, and one of us would hold him while the other climbed on. He was then let go, and was freed. He would pick up speed as he went out of the lot, and as soon as he was satisfied with his speed he would dig his hooves in the dirt, hold his head down, and stop. The rider had only one way to go . . . sliding down his neck.

When a bull goes into a roll, his skin also rolls some on his body, and a rider on his back has a problem until he gets off. A challenge is fun . . . sometimes. One Sunday it was my time to outsmart that bull, and we got ready. I got on, and J.P. let go. The bull took off and away we went. The gate was small. The gateposts were made of old railroad ties and had a good hold on the ground, and not ready to move when we went through. I had only a pair of pants on. My rib cage met a post, and the bull kept going, leaving me in the gateway. That was all for that day.

We went to church that night, and I went to sleep on the church bench. When church was over, Dad woke me up to go home, but he started talking to some man, and I, only half-awake, fell. The man felt sorry for me, but Dad said, "He's alright. You should see what a bull did to his side today! He's pretty tough!" My rib cage looked like I was whipped with a weed eater. I thought, "Man! If he thinks that that didn't hurt, he should have to wear my skin for awhile!"

The barnyard was a good place to play, even on a rainy day. We could get out of the house and out of Mama's and Daddy's way. Sometimes, we would have peanuts in the crib and enjoyed a good treat. We could sit and eat, or fill our pockets and be on our way and eat as we went. On these rainy days, I think we enjoyed killing rats and mice the most. The floor and the side were nailed on the sill on the back of the crib. The floor joist kind of made a boxed-in place where the rats would run when we got after them. Then we would get something to pry a board loose to try to get our hands in there. I remember one time when we did that, I ran my hand in there and grabbed a rat and threw him on the ground before it bit me. It didn't work every time. I always wanted to see his blood, not mine.

We had another way of killing rats and mice. We would go inside the crib, shut the door, settle down and not move for a while. The mice just couldn't stand there not knowing whether we were still there or not. They would come out from the pile of corn through a hole between the different ears, and then just sit there very still, just watching us. We wouldn't move till they went back down into the hole. We knew he would come back, so we put a rock in our sling shots. Pulling back the loaded pouch, and aiming at the hole that he came out through the first time. He might have been coming through another hole, but it would be close to the first hole. When he did, he would receive a package. Merry Christmas! He should have listened to Mama or Grandma Hodges, "Curiosity kills the cat." Remember?

We knew the mouse wouldn't be alone. Another one would take its place. Either the rats had more patience or were smarter, I don't know which. They would usually show up around some place away from the corn, but not always.

Sometimes kids like competition. They also like to win, and they do all that they can to do so. Where could we pass dirt and still stay clean? At the barn yard, of course, if dirt is cow manure that is. One of us would get the idea to make a run for it to the crib. The first one could stay, and the other one would fight from the ground. We had a stock pile laid up for that time. We used cow manure, but sometimes found mule manure that was about biscuit size and just right to throw. The one on the ground would run between the cows if they were there, while the one in the crib would duck away from the door way.

Did you know that when kids do things like that, the one on the receiving side would duck two times if he thinks that he is going to let loose, and is really just pretending. The receiver will not duck on the third time. Well, it worked at first. Wet corn cobs work too, but nobody wants to be hit with one of those. When we got through and were ready to clean up, the only running water was in the branch after the rain. I don't guess Mama cared too much for us to play where the cows had been.

One summer Dad told us that once they had planted popcorn, it was a good year and had made a big crop. They stored the popcorn in the loft in the barn above the mule stall. The weather turned hot, hot, hot, and that popcorn began to pop. It was flowing down around the mule. The mule looked up and probably began to think it was snow and he froze to death. I began to worry about my daddy, and now I find out that my grandkids worry about me.

Sometimes Alma Lee, J.P., and I would catch a horsefly and stick a straw in his rear. Then we would turn him loose and watch him go. We could see how far he went, while heading for the state line. Sometimes we would tie a string to the straw, if we knew where to find the string. We could see it better. We would enjoy the show, and the cows would enjoy the relief. The horseflies loved to eat on the cows. I wonder whatever happened to those flies once they became air born.

At the log house, where we lived at one time, there was a large barn with a board fence. It ran close enough that there was a good possibility that Alma Lee and I could climb up there and have some fun throwing bricks from the roof to the ground. It really worked. When we got up there, we didn't see J.P. climbing up after us. This is because the roof over lapped the fence enough that we missed something. When we started throwing bricks, one of mine made a connection with J.P.'s head. Uncle Preston was doing some work for Daddy and we saw him come out from the edge of the barn. He had J.P. in his arms, shaking him and trying to get him to catch his breath, or to come to, I don't know which. The blood was coming from his head freely. Mama and Daddy were gone. Preston took off to the doctor or somewhere, while Alma Lee and I stayed home alone. We didn't know we had any love for that four year old till then, but we had plenty of time to think, cry, and share our thoughts about what if he died. J.P left with a big towel wrapped around his head, but came back with a loss of some hair and a large bandage. Alma Lee and I got our orders to turn right and walk straight when the folks got home. We could walk through the barn, around it, but not on top of it. It was easy to remember not to walk on top of the barn again.

Once we had some young chickens that were cannibalistic. They would get behind one and start pecking until they would get the blood to show, and then the rest of them would start pecking on the same one. Then, it seemed that they all wanted in on the act, and most of them must have gotten in on it, because the one pecked sometimes would have a big hole pecked into its rear end.

Some said they needed some kind of chemicals, some said they were crowded up too much, but how do we keep them from bunching up? They were so bad and the ones getting pecked would soon die, so Mama would try to keep tar on the raw part, but had to separate them to stop it. If we eat dumb chickens, will that make us dumb?

With no money, and without borrowing money, the cows were not fed very well in the winter. They got fed just enough to keep them alive until the grass came out in the spring. Sometimes the cows would get sick. Back then, people would say that the cows had hollow horn or hollow tail. So people, including us, would get a file and hammer, then beat the file handle-end flat and use it to drill in the horns to relieve some of the pressure. Then the tail called for a slit about four inches or so on the end of their tail. We would fill it with salt till the hollow part was full. Then we would wrap it up in a towel till it grew back. Then there were times when we would pour out turpentine in a saucer, and hold it up to their navel and the turpentine would go in the cow. Other people just said that they had hollow stomach and needed more feed.

Sometimes we would feed the cows with some cut sweet potatoes or some kind of greens we were growing. Sometime the turnips needed cutting before feeding it to the cows. As kids, we might not have done a really good job. The cows would choke on it and our neighbors across the field would come over and help us get it out of their throat. They would put a horseshoe in their mouth, and stick an arm through it without getting bit. It worked really well. Some people believed giving cows sweet potatoes would dry them up, meaning that they would stop giving milk.

I once had a pig that I got for a 4-H membership to raise as a tool to learn, and of course, there is always a judging for prizes. This was my only chance to join, but I had no way for getting to the meetings. I had no way to know how to feed and care for it other than feed it out like any other hog. My hog was pretty, the first all white hog I had ever seen. That kind needs a lot of shade and plenty of water to lie in so it wouldn't get sunburned. Those hogs were easy to blister in the hot sun. I did very well in raising her and when she was ready to breed, Daddy took her to make things happen. She had eight little pigs. I wondered if that was some kind of record until someone told me of one sow bringing out thirteen little ones, so that burst my bubble. The sow only had them a short time when she got sick of something, we never knew what. I gave her whatever Mama gave me, but she died anyway. We had to use some of the cow's milk to feed the little ones for a few days.

People thought of a hog not having sweat glands and not being able to sweat was why they needed to be close to water to soak in, but that old sow was sweating before she died. I wondered about those sweat glands after that, and had no answer why she did sweat when she couldn't. I thought back, and I think she may have been in the hot sun while dying. Some said a snake may have bit her, but snakes weren't supposed to hurt a hog like that because their bodies know how to prevent it.

Daddy had a few hogs in the little patch just outside the barn lot. J.P. and I got ideas about being on one and seeing how far we could ride it. We took feed out to the patch. All around where the feed and water troughs were it was real nasty because of being wet and hog dung was mixed in that mud. When we put the feed out, the chickens were everywhere so they were where the hogs ate. They liked hog feed, too. Those chickens would ease up to the feed trough and wait until they felt safe to stick their head in without getting bit while also trying to keep from stepping in anything. We didn't raise any germ free hogs; we weren't germ free ourselves. Every time something came by, we caught it. Measles, seven-year-itch, pink eye and such, and now it was hogs we were to catch. When the chickens are watching where they step, it has to be bad! As long as we stayed on our feet, okay, but the fun was to see who could ride those hogs and stay clean the longest. The hogs were eating as fast as they could to keep the others from eating the most. The chickens were looking for a chance to peck up their fair share, staying alert to out-smart a hog, and keeping their feet clean as possible all at the same time. We boys were getting ready to jump astraddle of a hog we each had picked out, and the fun was on! The hogs would feel us jump on their backs, and with one quick jump from them, we were off very suddenly.

They would go back to eating, pretending not to notice us, but at the same time standing where one eye would be on us. We would try to outsmart the hogs to be able to ride on them, but all we could do was try again and again and again. Their skin was too tight and their hair was too short to get a handful to hold on. Why did we not think to put a rope around them and have something to hold on to? Well, we didn't know the rodeo people did that to the bulls. We never saw a rodeo, so how could two young boys think of something so smart? Now, if we had some training by someone who knew how to ride a hog and we stayed with it, we might still be riding hogs in the rodeo all over the country. If anybody got broken that day, it sure wasn't the hogs. I don't know now who stayed clean the longest, but all that hog fertilizer we had on us, we should have grown a lot larger than we did. Do hogs change? We did.

I guess being the oldest sibling is about as bad as being the youngest at times. I'll bet Alma Lee would admit to it if someone would have asked her about it. Once the oldest falls in love among the rest of the nest, they become kind of separated from the rest and no one to understand their plight in life, and have absolutely no pity. Life becomes a terrible state, and it seems that not much good comes to the person that is love sick between each visit to the two that is most important in each others' lives.

One day, when the lovers were out of the house, in the yard, and looking at one thing and thinking about something else, J.P. and I got their attention. They both had their eyes and mind on the same thing. What did we do? The mule was just outside of the lot in the edge of the field that was close to the house where Alma Lee and Gene were. We had done this before, but at the moment we did not have a thought about what was to happen. We got us some cow dab and begin to put that mule on the run. As she jumped, jerked and started off running at full speed, she let out gas every time her hind feet left the ground. We didn't think her exhaust line would be at work when we got the idea. The two lovers looked at each other with a sheepish look and J.P. and I looked at them with a hard-to-do smile, but we knew that we had goofed and so did Alma Lee and Gene.

Uncle Oren, as I mentioned earlier, lived down south around and in Moss Point. Someone he knew was supposed to have seen two small kid goats riding down the river on a log. It sounds to me that some boys may have pulled off pranks that boys do when they have an opportunity. That would sound like fun. Uncle Oren had the privilege of accepting the goats and asked Daddy if he wanted to raise them up on our farm. A goat will eat most anything so should not cost much to feed, and goat meat tastes good, so why not? There was a girl and a boy. They learned at an early age how to get the attention of people. They did a good job getting ours by acting like two hungry dogs. Every time we got out where they could get to us, they were there to pester us, following us around talking goat language, but I think what they were saying was, "You will never forget us, we will see to that."

By the tone of their voices, when we could hear one of them, we very well knew if we needed to go check on them. Like a dog, they would sound different at a different hope of attention. Usually, it would be a goat caught in a net wire fence behind the barn, where they liked to stick their heads out. Their horns wouldn't let them loose so they called for help. There were times we would start to pick up something from the ground and have to move a goat. Sometimes, just to walk, we would have to move them. When we were going out a while, we had to be sure the gate was closed between us and those pesky goats. They sure needed a mama and only they knew where they lost her. Since they wouldn't be able to find that place again, they thought everybody should take good care of them, I guess. We sure got tired of them and as we say, "They got our goat." We would have liked to see them go to, well, someplace away off.

One of them was always getting into Daddy's corn field. Daddy just couldn't figure how in the world that thing was able to get there when we had a good fence to keep them in. Daddy also had some hogs in the same fenced in area. I don't know just how many, but we never had much of a group at one time. The hogs got along very well with the goats, except when it was feeding time. You could hear a little fussing going on. The hogs enjoyed being in control and tried to eat more than any other mouth that tried to gobble up food. When the food was gone, they would walk around the trough very slowly, sniffing around to be sure the feed was really gone. Then, the goats and hogs were back to being friends again.

Sometimes a hog would smell around and pick up a little grass that looked good enough along the fence. A goat would be on the watch and see the hog getting closer to the fence; closer and closer until he saw the hog was in just the right place. He then jumped on the hogs back, over the fence, and into the corn. Now, the mystery came to an end when he got caught. He wasn't the only one on watch.

Once, I heard Grandpa Hodges tell Daddy that the way to make goat meat taste good was when skinning them to never let the hair touch the meat. If it did, it would taste too strong. Knox Walters was a man that ate anything different just to see what it tasted like, and told me polecat meat tastes sweet if it was skinned, not letting any hair touch the meat. Well, I really didn't intend to ever take the hair off the meat of a polecat. Neither was I ever going to eat the meat or the hair of one.

There was one chore around the house that the three of us, Alma Lee, J.P. and I liked to do. That was to go pick peas, butter beans and okra after they dried in the field and bring them into the yard. Then we would put them on some roofing tin that the hot, bright sun would really make hot in summer time. After we put the vegetables on it, some of the seed would pop out after getting hot. We would put the rest in a sack, which may be a few days later. The sack had to be burlap to do what we wanted. We would get a good stick, beat the sack for a few times, turn the sack over, and beat for awhile longer. We would turn it again and again, beating it each time until most of the shells of the peas or butter beans were opened (or the okra, whichever we were processing), pour them into a tub or bucket, put another tub on the ground, and then get up in a chair or something to make us high and catch the wind right. We would then pour the seed from the one bucket into another bucket on the ground. As we did this, the seed, being heavier than the shell, would fall straight into the tub as the shells would be carried away by the wind. Okra was different, but easy to get separated, because the seed would go to the bottom of the pile of hulls. To keep weevils out, we would store the seed in fruit jars until the next planting season. Now, if we were saving seed from the fruit of a vine, like watermelons, cantaloupe, pumpkin or such, we would dry them the same way, but separate the inner part from the seed and store those seeds the same way in a jar. We also tried drying some peaches that we sliced up, and it did alright. We enjoyed them until we saw where the flies had gotten to them and little worms were coming from them. That was the end of that. Those worms were not on the list for our diet.

Daddy smoked back in our early years. Then there was not much known about cancer, except no one wanted it, and if people with it were operated on they didn't live long. People would say that when the doctor opened somebody up, the oxygen would get to the cancer and it would go wild. Then the patient would die soon, but no one knew what caused it. So most men smoked, and boys like to do things their daddies do. J.P. and I were no different, so we did experiment some with some kinds of leaves usually, and the grape leaves were my choice. Somebody said some special vines in the swamps were good, but I didn't like smoking the vines, even though it had small holes through the vine and was easy to pull smoke through it.

I remember I was outside the front gate once when I lit up, and J.P. hollered something like, "I hear Daddy." I ran with my cigarette in my hand heading toward the branch down the road, close enough to the house I could throw a rock from the house and hit the branch. As I ran around the corner of the fence, Daddy drove right toward me. I didn't want to get caught, nor did I know what to do, so I closed my hand with my smoke in it. The fire went out, and I was lucky not to be burnt.

Another time, J.P. had a nickel and spent it on a plug of chewing tobacco. He came home, showed it to me, and we both had a chew. J.P. started getting sick and when it started to come up, J.P. offered it to me. I was so glad he got sick so I could chew the entire plug myself. We had a good idea. We thought of drying it and making a smoke, but it didn't dry very well so we chewed it.

We also tried rabbit tobacco leaves but couldn't do much with it, smoking or chewing. If we couldn't make it work, how did it get its name Rabbit Tobacco? That stuff doesn't even dry very well.

Around the house, we had a bad odor for several days. When it started, if we were outside the house, the bad smell would follow us into the house. Daddy went out looking for the problem and found it in the branch that ran around side of the house. The branch started out back of the field where the gap is and the two bays start. One bay went north and one went south, but the branch went west. Well, remember we lived down at the foot of the hills, and sometime, long ago, all that water finally had to find its own way to the river. The branch itself developed different kinds of growth, including some kind of heavy vines with thorns on it, and it was hard to go through or in between them. When Daddy found the source of the stench, this is what he saw. A cow had foundered in the under growth, including the briers, and was dead. He looked over the situation, and he saw how big she was and how thick the growth was. Even though we had a lot of buzzards around at the time, he thought he could just burn her up by placing a lot of wood around her and build a good fire in the pile of wood before all those buzzards could solve the problem. He had looked for that cow before, because she had been missing for several days, but this time he found her very easily. We know if we have a steak on the stove the aroma can cheer us up, but as soon as it is eaten, the good smell is gone. Not so when a cow is lying in a heavily wooded spot and on a wet ground with burning wood around her. The fire needed to be under her in a dry place with plenty of wood to keep it going, and besides that, there was plenty of water to dry up that was in the cow before she was done. That is a lot of meat to cook up at once, and my daddy didn't have that much wood on the fire. The buzzards had to just sit out there and wait for lunch to cool off before they could help. Now I don't think my daddy did the right thing because there were several days before that smell disappeared from our forty acres, our bedroom, living room, kitchen, and dining room. There are things in life that each of us wish we could just forget and all would change, but it doesn't happen in this world. The memory sometimes lasts a long time. Many years later, this memory was brought back when I was in war and smelled the bodies of many dead men.

Around the Church

The visit to church never changed much as I remember it. The church was the church, like the dinner was the dinner, and we know about what will happen even before we go, but sometimes . . . Well, let's see if I remember anything different ever happening.

I remember we had a baptism in Third Creek. That is across Tallahala from where the church and the members thought they could put a dam across the draw that headed up beside the building, or a few yards away, actually. The first big rain blew the dam out, and I think there may have been too much sand in the soil. I don't know why it didn't hold, but no more dam.

Daddy's brother drank a little spirits sometimes, and one evening he went into the church while under the influence. Back then, we had a problem with the seven year itch. That evening, we had a visiting preacher that knew too few people there. A couple of girls, and I don't remember who but one whose name was Jewel and maybe her sister, was with my uncle, and tried to calm him down. He finally got up and walked out with the girls following behind. The preacher stopped preaching long enough to speak out saying, "Come back in when you get through scratching." The members that knew him had something to laugh about.

Two boys, who were brothers and ran together, were in church one night, and one was sleeping with his head back and was snoring. James Ross was in his teens, and at the age to have fun at every opportunity. He had a wadded up gum wrapper. He leaned over and dropped it in the snoring boy's mouth. The boy began coughing, snorting, making faces and raised his head, swallowed it and went back to sleep. I don't think the pastor saw it happen because he didn't laugh or stop preaching.

Once we had a baptism going on at Third Creek. The program was going on and when it came time for prayer, two boys said, "Let's go!" and started running while all the others had their heads down. I headed their way. As I started by, one of Daddy's brothers, Elton, reached out to stop me but said nothing, nor did he have to, nor did he have to hold me. That was one of the things I had never done because I knew better. That was a lesson that stuck with me. I never did that again. After about sixty years, I told him about the lesson that he taught me that stuck, and he could not remember it.

Wednesday nights. I remember one Wednesday night when Daddy and I went to church, and I think the family was there. After church, Daddy and the pastor were putting a light in the podium. Of course, I couldn't hear what they were saying. I wondered for many years why they would do that, then just close the door and leave for the night. I asked Daddy maybe forty years later why they did that, thinking I was going to hear some ancient tradition. Now, he couldn't remember anything about that. How terrible; a memory that will never do anyone any good.

Daddy went to Wednesday night service alone one night. As he was walking on Highway 29, which at the time was a gravel state highway, he was playing with a 22 cartridge he had with him. At the time, he smoked a pipe. He got his tobacco out, filled his pipe, packed it down, struck a match, and lit his pipe. As he was walking along, the pipe blew up. He wiped the trash from his face, got down on his knees, and by the light of the moon, he picked up all the parts he could find. When he got home, he used wire to hold all the parts together. Somehow, that cartridge got into his pipe from his pocket, and he never figured how it happened but he was, as I said, playing with it before he put tobacco in. Now, how did all that happen? He went to the Carpenter Grandparent's house. He still had brothers that were living at home so he told them about his pipe, as he was still using it and they had a big laugh out of it. They pitched in and bought him a new pipe. I tried to figure how he didn't get his face torn up. I'm glad he didn't.

Let us talk about seeing the unseen. I did just that when I was almost home from Wednesday church one night when I had gone alone. The road I was on was more of a cow trail than a wagon road in one place, and there had been a large oak tree cut down that the trail went around. As I approached the stump, there was a bright but soft light that shown all around me in a flash, a light I had not ever seen before and it gave me a fright that got a grip on me. I looked back to the road behind me, thinking to run because whatever it was could outrun me, so I walked very quickly toward home. All were asleep when I reached my destination so I had to wait until the next day before I could tell anyone about my experience. Alma Lee was in Runnelstown the next day, and people were talking about a star falling someplace near Runnelstown as they were sitting on their porch. Sometimes we can learn a lot going to church.

I guess one of the things I remember about church most is dinner on the grounds. Not that I enjoyed eating more than anything else, but to be with other kids and play together. There were several large pine trees south and southeast of the church that made a good shade, and close enough to nail tables together from tree to tree. Of course, we had no air condition except hand held fans that some funeral home had donated, and yet we were accustomed to the heat for we never knew anything different from our summer time weather. Besides, who cared if the summer was hot and we were wet with sweat when we got to church with all the highway dirt stuck to our wet clothes? The people of the church would cook the food. A lot of us had to walk long distances with the food to church. Of course, we had never heard of the Health Department, refrigerators, or someone getting food poison. All we had were towels to throw over the food to keep the dirt and flies off. The church was off the ground, and kids could crawl under it if they wanted to. The best place was where kids could run and chase each other. The drinking water was across the road in the schoolyard. It ran from an Artesian well into a trough where people could water their mules, and could control the flow so there would be no mud hole around there. We could stand and eat, bring our chairs from home in a wagon or buggy (if we had one) or if someone had a car that would work, or even sit on the ground. I don't remember, but I suppose some ate inside the church;

maybe the older people. Some had table cloths or sheets to put on the ground. Flies were plentiful, and so were the ants. There was a lot of fellowship with people we would not see for another week.

I was in church one night, sleeping very soundly, when the pastor ended his sermon, the singing stopped, and the closing prayer shut down. The people got up to either visit or go home. I was woken up to go home. I was trying to stay awake so I could stand up long enough to be able to walk home when all the visiting was finished. I looked up, and there was my mama talking to someone with her back to me. I knew her without seeing her face because of her build, the long coat she had on and I could hear her voice. I reached up and all sleepy eyed, patted her on the back side and she kept talking. I wanted to go home and go back to sleep. Soon Mama stepped out to where she could see me and I see her. Oops! I had been patting Mrs. Sanford on the back side instead of my mama! I never knew they looked alike from behind, and I didn't even know they felt so much alike from behind. How did they find a blue coat just alike? I couldn't face her anymore that night even though she said she thought I was one of her kids because that was the way they did her, also. That was a night when I just couldn't leave the church quick enough.

Around The House

A home out of the city is not a home without also having a dog, so most of the time we had a dog. Not often, but sometimes, a friend would come to our house and would have a dog with him. If the dogs were close to the same size, and we started getting bored, we would catch the dogs and rub their noses together and the fight started; that is until we saw Mama coming or saw blood, whichever came first. It was like a ball game. It was a good feeling to have a dog that won the fight, but we also knew, regardless who won, we had lots of fun.

As a young boy, we were hardly ever bored, unless it was while we were working and we needed to quit so that we could play. I did feel I may be allergic to work, and we had a lot to play with that didn't cost money. One thing that stuck with me was a Chinaberry tree in our back yard. When the berries got to full size, we would get a fishing cane, sizing up the right section of the cane that the berries would fit into pretty tightly. We would fix up a stick like a dowel pin to use as a plunger. Once we had the right size, we would put a berry in each end of the tube we made from the cane, and push one berry into the tube with the plunger. After the pressure built up, the other berry would pop out. Once we got everything right, the race was on! We tried to shoot each other on the run.

Most of our toys were homemade by hand. For clean fun, we would take a corn cob, stick three or four feathers in one end, throw it up into the air, and watch it go around and around until it hit the dirt. Sometimes, we would want a dart to throw at a wood target and try to stick it in a bull's eye. We could do that, too. We would take a sage straw, about five inches long, put a Victrola needle in one end, and put small strips of paper on the other end to make it go around and around, plus go straight to the target. Now we were ready for a dart board!

J.P. and I made our sling shots to shoot rocks, arrows or crab apples. We made our fishing lines out of number eight thread. We would twist it and hang the middle of the line on something like a limb just to hold it until we could bring both ends together, until we got it ready to turn loose to wind it together. It makes a strong fishing line and it works, too.

We have made our own so-called pistol using a piece of wood cut in the shape of a pistol. We would attach a clothes pin on the back of the handle, take a tire tube, and make a rubber band from the tube. We had something to shoot at each other with. Now we were at war again.

For a little racket, we sometimes found a food can and put a small hole in the bottom, ran a string through the hole, and tied a knot on it so that when you pulled it, the string wouldn't slide through the can. We waxed the string, closed the thumb and finger around it and as we pulled, we let the string slip through our finger. Now we had some racket from a Dumb Bull.

At Christmas time, we had other uses for a tin can. One was driving a nail in the bottom of the can the size of a fire cracker. We would drive the can a little way into the ground where it would be a little tight, stick a fire cracker almost all the way in with the fuse sticking out, and light it. After just a moment, up into the air it would go!

Now when we ran out of firecrackers, we did the same with the can as before. Only this time we would use a carbide can because it needed to be a can that can be closed tight with a push down lid, not one with a screw down type lid. We took a nail, put a hole in the bottom of the can, put a grain of carbide in, and followed it with a small amount of water to form gas. Then we would set it down and push the lid on tight, put light to the hole in the bottom and away went the lid! Now Christmas has lasted a little longer!

J.P. and I learned how to make a bird trap. Using sticks nailed or tied with string to hold the sticks together, to make a box like trap with a three piece trigger to throw the trap. It worked, too.

The boys in the community had a game with tops. We would decide who was to spin their top first in a circle on the ground. While it was still spinning, everyone else would try to spin their top on the one in the circle while it was still spinning to try to break it. I thought I could make a top, and if it broke it wouldn't be as bad as if I spent money for it. I did make one, and it worked, too, but not as good as a store bought top.

We would find a wasp nest and just couldn't ignore it. Besides that, fish like those little worms inside the nest.

We would either set fire to some paper or throw what were usually clods of dirt at it. We knew when we got chased, we could run a little way, lay flat on the ground, and let wasps fly over us and go tend to their business. Sometime it would work, but I don't know why. Maybe their babies were crying out for the mothers, and we couldn't hear it as their mothers could. I have no answer to the mystery.

Mr. Broadhead taught us boys how to have a little fun using chickens. We would get a small stick and make a small split in it. When we would pull it apart just a little, it would spring back. We would catch a chicken and pull the split open enough to slide it up on the tail enough to catch a little meat instead of all feathers. As Mr. Broadhead said, she would think a snake had her, and she would jump up and down a few times. If it didn't come off, she would head down through the bushes until it did come off. Would we call that chicken hopping or a chicken dance?

We kids learned we could get a steel band, like a wagon wheel, to hold the center of the wheel together or the same size of band. We would take a piece of wood, about one inch by two inches by about maybe three feet long, with a cross piece at the bottom to push the band as we went running with the band rolling along being pushed. That was our car.

Mama did a lot of sewing, and when she finished spools of number eight thread we liked to play with them. We learned we could get a rubber band, a short piece of sage straw about five inches long, and some soap. Put it all together and we would have our tractor.

Alma Lee was good about making out new plans to keep us busy, but not all the things we did made everybody happy. Mama had gotten mad at us because we didn't give the peaches time to get ripe before we started eating them. She laid down the law that we were to let them ripen before we ate anymore. Alma Lee had an idea. We were to let the peaches stay on the tree, bite off a little and leave the rest. Mama would think it was the chickens and we would still have peaches to eat. When Mama saw what was hanging on the tree, she looked us up. When she confronted us, we told her the chickens did it. She told us she had never seen a chicken with teeth. She played the role of school teacher and she did a good job because I still remember the lesson she taught us. What good is an idea if it hasn't been tried? It just didn't work.

Alma Lee could always think of so many good things to do. She asked me what I thought about putting a peanut on a string and then tying the string on the grape vine under the harbor to see what the chickens would do. That we did; we backed away, sat down and waited. The curiosity of a chicken! We had the peanut maybe three feet off the ground, and the chicken had to jump up to reach it. They looked as if they were having a good time, so we put up several more so more chickens could be involved. One day, we were having more chicken fun until Mama called us in for lunch. We forgot our entertainment was still going on, and we didn't take down the peanuts. After we ate, we were off to someplace else. Later, Mama got our attention, got up to us, and face to face told us that there was a dead chicken hanging on a string that had a peanut on it. Because of her, we never had that fun again. We felt bad the chicken swallowed the peanut, and couldn't un-swallow it, but hanged there and died.

Are your feet breaking out with open sores, closed sores or sore sores? J.P. and I learned from Mama to boil red oak bark, take the water while it was still hot, and soak your feet for a while and it brings about healing. I don't know what red oak has in it that brings about healing, but it works.

Rubber was used for different things before synthetic rubber. As I mentioned: making a toy gun with it; using it for our tractor made of spool, rubber, stick and soap; used for chair bottoms; springs for yard gates to keep the gate closed; save worn out shoes soles; make sandals; strips of rubber to tie fishing poles together and such to go floating in the lake we used tubes blown up; weather strips for doors; and we kids used rubber strips to pull back and hurt flies. I think today if we had rubber trees along the highways and a car went out of control and hit a tree, the car would just bounce back. Then the driver could crank it up, and go on without being hurt, that is if his head didn't pop off in the accident.

Daddy made brooms for the house at times, not all the time. When he did it saved money and gave him something to do. We had what we called broom sage that grew good close by. Daddy used to make brooms for sweeping the dirt and sand from the house. Now they didn't do a good job like a store bought broom, but after all, we were on hard times.

Now to scrub the floors, Daddy made a push broom. He made a block of wood, I am guessing about twelve inches long, three or four inches wide, about two inches thick, and used a brace and bit to drill holes close together to use corn shucks stuck into the holes, wedging them where they wouldn't come out. He put a handle on it and with the lye water and some soap, it was ready to scrub dirty places off the floor like any other push broom. Dirt didn't have a chance.

To get rid of bed bugs when we moved from one house to another, which was only a few times, we kids watched Mama wash the cracks in the walls and floor with lye water to kill the bed bugs so when we lie on the bed we wouldn't get eat up by those little suckers. In the summer time, we kids and Mama would put the mattresses out in the sun to kill them and turn the mattress over in about a half of a day.

After years passed on, I asked Mama what ever happened to the bed bugs because I had not seen or heard about them in a long time. She said that when the roaches moved into the houses, they ate the bed bugs. Another mystery solved.

I learned from Daddy how to care for potatoes after they are harvested. Irish potatoes were dried in the sun until there is no moisture on them. Then take dried pine needles, put them in the loft of the barn, then lay the potatoes on top of them; but you have to eat them soon. They didn't last long.

To winter sweet potatoes, Daddy dug dirt, built a mound high enough the rain water wouldn't reach the potatoes, and put pine needles on top of the mound. Then he would then prepare a doorway using a piece of roofing tin for the door, put potatoes in and as the potatoes went in so did the straw. The straw and the dirt helped insulate, and the dirt held everything together. Then he put some roofing tin on top to keep the dirt from washing off. The door was also fixed to keep out rats who also like the taste of good potatoes.

We didn't have money to buy soda pop, but we did better than that. We had a lot of good old sassafras growing all around, and we sometimes needed to dig some of that out of fence rows or just most any place around the house.

We would throw the stuff away anyway, so why not use it? That is one drink that would make a kid stay around the house. We had it already, and we dug it up for free. We had a well with plenty of water that was just waiting for someone to draw out of the well at no cost. We had stove wood that cost only a little energy to cut it and take it into the house. When we had something cooking, we would already have a fire to add wood to so we needed no matches to start the fire. If it weren't for the sugar that went into it that stuff, it sure would be good and cheap for a good tasting drink. It was also suppose to be a good blood medicine. By the way, when root beer became one of our sodas on the market it sure made a big hit in South Mississippi. It tasted a lot like sassafras tea!

Why do I mention matches? Well, we kept a little fire going on all the time since wood was plenty, and we had no money for matches for some time. The grandparents' also had a fire going all the time. If our fire went out, some of us would go over to their house and bring back a stick with some hot coals on it to start our fire again. They lived almost a half mile from us so we had to be careful how we carried it home.

Uncle Leon was a merchant marine and his ship was in some country. I don't remember where it was because I didn't go much farther than Hattiesburg back then, so the foreign countries meant nothing to me. He got a hold of a small monkey, hid it on the ship, and tried to keep it quiet so no one heard or saw the thing. To sneak monkeys into the United States was a "no-no". He made it back and took it home, which was close to us, for the kids and wife to play with. It was a lot of fun. J.P. and I would go over to their house and make out like we were whipping Beulah, Uncle Leon's wife. We would be inside the house with the monkey looking in through the screen door. That would make the monkey so mad that he would try to get inside the house to get us. He had some sharp teeth, too!

Beulah had a cat and I think maybe four kittens, and the monkey would take them up in a pine tree in the yard and play with them. They would squall, but that monkey didn't seem to hear a thing. One by one, he would leave the kittens up in the tree, and one by one, each would end up falling out of the tree. They were so high up when they fell, they all died; all because of that monkey.

Uncle Leon sold the monkey to Daddy, and when we got it home we started feeding it dried raisins which he liked. We never thought about when those raisins filled his stomach they would call for water and swell the poor little fellow up and kill him with the stomach ache. We tried hard with Mama's help to save the poor fellow. He was hurting badly, but we couldn't do anything that would help him. Alma Lee, J.P. and I cried and felt sorry for ourselves, probably more than the poor animal.

We had a funeral for him, and he was buried under a cedar tree in the front of the house. He was put in a shoe box. Years later, Uncle Leon wanted his skeleton and was going to dig him up. He never did find him. I guess the poor thing escaped.

Mama would have us three kids, Alma Lee, J.P. and me sit around her as she read the Bible. It was a joy when she took her time and left room for questions if any of us wanted to understand something. There is one thing I remember about her and Bible time. She would explain the Jews' place in the entire Bible, before we were old enough to form our own ideas about the cross and the killings. She told us that we should keep an open mind when we studied the Bible, the people, the times and their culture.

In later years, I heard her say that we had only two books in the house back then. One was the Bible, and one was the *Esquire Child's Book*. She explained when she read the Bible, that the Bible was the history of our religion and a true book. *The Esquire Book* was fiction so we would learn the difference at a young age. She tried to teach us the things that had happened, were happening, and the things to come. My mama and daddy were good Christian parents. That is more than a lot of people had and wish they had.

There is a company in Laurel, Mississippi, that makes Masonite. This is a kind of fiberboard made from pressed wood fibers, used in building material, insulation, etc. I don't know how long they have made Masonite, but I remember as a small boy they made it. As years have passed by, there has been some upgrading that lets them produce a better product, better way of disposing of the waste, and probably other improvements to better them. In the early years, the company turned the waste loose down the old Tallahala River that came within around a mile from our home. If the wind was from the west, many times the stench was bad. No one I know ever looked forward to enjoying a good whiff of the bad odor.

The fish died for many miles from the wood fibers that were in the waste, as it clogged up their breathing. Many people ran down to the river when they received word that the waste was on its way and caught fish that came up, but the dead ones they let float on by. Some caught what they could use for a few days, and kept them by salting then down after cleaning them, then put them in a safe in the kitchen where the stove was. The safe was a kitchen cabinet with screened doors to keep out flies.

Some people would get a load, head to town, and sell them until the law found them. The way they had prepared them to get them to Hattiesburg was put them in the bed of a pickup truck with ice packed around them. Others took them home and salted them down in a barrel or a wood box. Remember, there were no refrigerators.

The company used screen wire in processing Masonite, yet only could use the wires once. They would then dispose of it, using new wire for each batch. Daddy found out that he could buy some of it very cheap so he got enough for our house. Before we got that, we didn't do so well at keeping out mosquitoes. When the mosquitoes got too bad, we would build a fire up wind to the house, and used green wood so there would be a lot of smoke. All the windows would be opened wide at evening time to prepare for the night. No, it wasn't good, but that was all we had at the time. We sure couldn't hit all of those things with our fly swatter, which was made with rubber from car tire tubes with a handle attached to it. That is the first I can remember any screen wire that people could actually nail over a window. Thank God for screen wire and Gulf Spray a little later!

I think that most of us have heard the phrase "beauty is in the eye of the beholder." Well, people use to dress up a fireplace by taking a piece of Masonite, card board or whatever could be used to cover the fire place, which was done often. One reason was because of Chimney Sweeps. These are birds that would go into the chimney and upset the soot, and of course the mess would find its way into the house. Some called the birds Chimney Swallows. How did people make a beautiful spot from the fire place? They would look in magazines for pretty pictures and paste on whatever they used covering up the hole.

In the yard, we had no lawn mower so to make it look good we used a hoe. The grass had to go. The flowers were rearranged to beautify the outside of the home. The floors were swept every day and needed it because with no grass, no shoes, no concrete, it felt good to not walk across the floor without having to wipe our feet on the bed.

One reason the knees in our overalls were worn out is we two boys would get down in the dirt to make roads and bridges for running our cars. These would be medicine bottles, hair tonic bottles or whatever would make the best tracks in the dirt. Under the house was a good place because of less hot sun and not many ants to get in our road way. Who wants to hurt an ant? We didn't throw away a good pair of britches just because they had a patch on the knee. It had to have a few patches, and some of them were to patch a patch. It was when the cloth was thin enough that it would not hold the thread that they would be thrown out. But in the yard is where a lot of fun is found for a child, even though it is hard on old clothes.

For a few years when people would buy things like feed, sugar and fertilizer, it would come in a fabric sack. With these sacks, women could make dresses, shirts and sometimes under clothes. Fertilizer sacks didn't go over too big because it had some kind of little knots in part of the fibers that make up the fabric. I don't remember after so many years, but I do know people used lots of starch and that may be the reason for that kind of sacks being bad about scratching the skin. Also, there was no color to the sacks but a dingy white.

The feed sacks had different patterns in print, so sometimes a person could kind of look through the sacks and pick out what looked good. Women had a chance to outdo each other in church when Sunday came. They could show off what they had made anyplace else they went. Now, can you visualize women going to a mercantile store and throwing sacks of feed around on the floor, trying to find the prettiest sacks to make the prettiest clothes with? Can you visualize the merchant standing there wondering how to be nice while stopping the women from making a mess without making them mad because they needed the people's trade and they did not want to lose their husband's business? The women needed to be able to sew well because of their financial problems in those years. Otherwise, they may have to cut two holes in the bottom of the sack, crawl into it, and put straps on to hold the thing on.

Not my mama. She was good in anything she did, from raising us kids to making clothes. She was good at changing sacks into clothes and not clothes into sacks. They looked good in church and anyplace else.

The ladies shared where to buy sacks and what kind the store had. When they were in the store they picked out which sack, not which feed. With the finished product, the ones with dresses and those with shirts, wherever they went, were happy and so were the chickens. "Where did you buy your sack?" were the common words around for a few years. The clothing store people probably felt cheated when those sacks begin walking around the front of their doors.

In a four room house, the rain or cold moved in and all the family was stuck inside the house. It became different than a home at times. Mama would have to bring order and quiet among us. We had to entertain ourselves some way. There were no books to read, no radio to play, and no television to turn on so we would play checkers, Jacks, dolls or something else, and there were things to make noise with. Now, that was something Mama got enough of pretty soon; noise.

Sometimes, it would be a leaf or blade of grass. We would hold our hands cupped together in a prayer motion with the thumbs together with the grass or leaf held firm between them and blow, making noise to get rid of the quietness that Mama enjoyed so much. Sometimes, it would be something else we would think up for noise. We would get tired of being nice and yet still wanted to be good for a while, but we still had Mama's ideas. A comb with a piece of paper over the teeth of it could be used to hum a tune. That was fun. When Mama got tired of that, she would have us play a quiet game like using a button with a size number 8 thread through two holes that were across from each other as a two hole button, stick a finger of one hand in one end of the thread that had been tied together as a loop, and a finger of the other hand in the other end. We would swing the button that was on the middle part, making the thread twist around itself, then pull both ends to make the button go around, let off slack to let the thread twist together the other way. It was somewhat like a yo-yo. It helped keep us busy.

Later years in summertime, J.P. and I used the rainy days in the corn crib to kill rats. Alma Lee didn't like killing rats so the poor girl had to stay in the house on those good old days.

When the frogs started singing, it was to me real music, especially going to bed when everyone was ready for a good night's rest. They were good little entertainers. That was mostly when the weather was wet and it was nighttime. Some said they were calling for more rain, but I think they were lonely and wet. The rain came and so did the frog eggs, in water spots and sometimes even cow trails. J.P. and I would play with that slime with wonder. Some said toads were good fish bait, but when we set out poles with toads on the line, we went back just to see the frog had crawled up the line and was setting on the pole waiting for us to come back. We never tried that again.

Our house must have wanted some excitement once in a while, and one of those times was when Joan was a small baby. As we were running around getting ready to get water on top of the house to put out a fire, I ran inside to grab Joan and lay her on the front porch. That way, if we lost the house we would have her where it would be easy to get her away from the fire. Mama came by the porch, picked her up, and put her away from the house. We got the fire out with the help of the Travis' that heard us hollering. After the scare was over, Mama and Alma Lee picked on me about putting Joan where we could watch her burn, but with the smile on their faces I knew they were kidding. After all, on the ground and in the grass is where the critters like ants, gnats, spiders, and cats always are. We love you, sis!

Sometimes the seven-year-itch would break loose in our school, and of course, we kids just had to get it. Man, when we scratched it that felt good, but made it worse. We lived in a partly log house during one of those episodes, and Mama had been using sulfur to heal the stuff that took over between the fingers worse than anyplace else, but new stuff came out on the market that had an unpleasant smell to it that bothered us. We would be alone in the house and wipe the medication off onto the logs of the house. When Mama found where we had been, she stopped being that sweet sugar Mama to being a salt healing mad Mama. You know salt heals, but it does hurt. This was Alma Lee and me; not J.P. that time.

Christmastime was good for us kids, but after we were old enough to be told there was no Santa Claus it made Christmas much like any other day. Santa Claus was always a mystery, and Mama and Daddy were always either up or getting up as soon as we woke up and started looking for the mark of a Santa Claus around the house. Mama would point out each of our presents if there was anything that didn't fit in the stocking. I always wondered just how in the world Mama knew which was ours, and Daddy must have known she was right because he would be laughing, enjoying Christmas by watching us. Mama would say, "This one is Alma Lee's. Marvin, this is yours. J.P., this one is yours." It seemed to be something between Mama and Santa Claus, because there were no names on anything, but we knew which stocking each one of us hung up.

After being told that there was no Santa, I believed it. Santa didn't come to see me anymore. I wondered later if I still believed he was real, would he have come back. Maybe he would still come now, at the old age that I am now.

The rain, cold and days without school gave us a job inside the house. Quilt making. Mama would set up the quilting frames by hanging them from the ceiling and put in a piece of material the size she wanted the quilt to be, carefully spread a thin layer of fresh ginned cotton, then the top Mama had pieced together when time would not be good for anything else. It took many days in the making, but when it was finished, lasted many years in the using. It was a good feeling to the young to look at the finished product and be able to say, "I helped to make that."

Mama woke me up one night and told me there was something after the chickens in the chicken house. I got up in fear that there may be someone out there in the dark. I got the shotgun and started easing out through the tall weeds with Mama several feet behind me, saying later it was because if someone jumped me she could jump them. I still wonder about that. I got to the chicken house, lit the carbide light as quickly as I could and jumped in where the chickens were, but no one was there. Mama eased in behind me, and we saw nothing but the chickens. The old hen made no racket while we were there. As we were ready to go back in our house, Mama looked up at the sill up over the door. When Dad built the building he left a little space between each board, and a board had a notch cut in the edge of it. There was our mystery. A hen saw the notch as she was about to sit down for the night, stuck her head through it to look around. As she sat down her neck slid down into the crack, but her head had to go back up to the notch before it would be able to get released. She thought she was caught, not having any brains. I promised Mama I would fix that hole when it was daylight. I don't remember if I did.

There was another night Mama woke me up to tell me someone was in another chicken house which was just a few feet from the backdoor. I got the gun, the carbide light, charging it in the dark, got a match, and we eased out to the chicken house. I lit the carbide light and shined it inside as quickly as I could and there it was; a civet cat. Now a civet cat is a small skunk that has its stripes going around it instead of down its back. He was standing there looking at me, as if to say my timing was bad. With one hand, I stuck the gun out the best I could and with the other hand I held the light too close to the end of the gun barrel, blasting that varmint. It wasn't a clean shot and to keep that thing from getting out in case I missed him, Mama shut the door and latched it. I told Mama I had no more matches, and she hesitated for a moment before letting me out. By that time the cat was dead, and I wore its perfume for a few days. Why didn't she give me heck that time like she did when J.P. and I helped the dog get a skunk out of a gopher hole? He had already killed two chickens by biting them on the neck and sucking their blood out.

I had been plowing one day with our old mule and had brought her to the backyard to where the well was to give her a drink before taking her in for the night. When the mule finished drinking, I jumped up on her back to ride her to her resting place under the barn for the night. J.P. must have had a memory of the barn and the brick hitting him in the head so many years back because as I started off for the free ride, J.P. picked up a corn stalk, after not seeing what he really wanted, and planted it on the mule's rump. She lifted up her front end, came down on her back-end, and went like a rocking horse. I lay on the ground. J.P. thought I was going to whip him so he ran up a ladder on top of the house. I don't think I ever knew he did this to me until many years later.

J.P. and I were kind of like cats; if anything moved, we caught it or shot at it. We liked to catch bugs. At night we ran down lightening bugs (or fireflies). They were always a mystery to me. Even now, I don't understand them. We had the pleasure of chasing them in the dark, and if we squeezed them, their light would still shine. Then there were doodlebugs, as we called them, which actually are a larva from the ant lion I think. We would move sand from his nesting place or trap, and if he was there he had to move to see if he had lunch in his trap; and we were watching.

We caught jacks with a straw. He would be a white worm with a large, orange head and pinchers at his mouth, and we would put the straw in his hole. He would get the straw, pushing it up to get it out of his hole, and we would see it move and were ready.

Then there were lizards, frogs, snakes, rats and grasshoppers, plus things I will think of later.

We had a smokehouse in the backyard, a wash pot to heat the water to kill a hog, and put a barrel in a slant in the ground to scald him. No, we didn't kill the hog with hot water, but put him in the hot water after he is dead. We turned the hog over changing ends in order to scald the skin to make the hair come out. There was a pole that ran through the smokehouse and stuck outside where we could hang the hog to cut the body open and apart. Then, it was carried into the house and prepared to hang in the smokehouse. The inner parts were cooked up: things like the liver, heart, head and lights, which were the lungs, etc. We boys were given some of the lean meat, which was good.

We killed hogs when the weather was cold. The flies were not out getting on the meat and the meat didn't get too warm before getting it taken care of. All this makes me wonder. First, we kill the hog and eat it, and then we clog up our system with all that hog lard and die. That means we got killed by the hog. Second, does that mean that when we get to heaven, those hogs will be waiting at heaven's gate laughing at us because they killed us last, which gives them the last laugh?

Is all that bad to eat raw? Just think about when I was small, there was no baby food as we have it today. People would chew food, take it out of their mouth, and put it in a baby's mouth because babies don't have teeth. That sounds bad, but when two people sleep together and face one another, one will breathe out and the other will breathe in and take the air from one body to the other. Can we call that regurgitated air? Which is worse?

Cecil and Elton were in their teens. I'm not sure their ages, but that put me a small boy just enjoying being at Grandma's house. The guys were telling us little ones that they could weigh people without scales. I knew how we weighed cotton at cotton harvest time and didn't believe them. To prove what they said they took Wilber, had him stand with his back to Elton and with his knees bent where Elton could bend over, grab him in his arms around Wilber's legs at the back of his knees with his bottom next to Elton's body. Elton picked him up and raised Wilber up then down a few times, then set him down and told him how much he weighed. Then they talked me into letting them weigh me. I was stupid back then, too, and finally agreed that it would be ok. Elton reached down and got me up, raised and lowered me a few times then stooped down to set me down only after Cecil slipped a pan of water between Elton's legs where I couldn't see what was going on behind me. As he was about to release me, he set me in a pan of water, right on my setter. That's when my three uncles found out that I had a big temper. What can a kid do?

Back to when I was four years old. I write this stuff down as I think about it. We lived in Harvey one year just across the Leaf River from Hattiesburg. One night, Alma Lee was washing dishes. It looked like she was having fun and I wanted to help. Mama said no. I was upon the kitchen counter watching Alma Lee and saw a little jar that had something white in it, got some on a spoon, and tasted it. The stuff in the jar was lye. I started hurting something bad, crying, hollering and jumping around. Mama and Daddy jumped up and went to rescue me. When they found what was wrong, I think they fed me hog lard or something to make me throw up, then fed me buttermilk and took me to the doctor. He said Mom and Dad did the best they could have done. I don't think any got past my tongue. From then on, my Mama made me wash dishes until the draft board rescued me.

A city man was making his rounds, trying to get a sale on some farm paper. It was wet from a good rain, and the road to our house was a dirt road and a real mess. J.P. and I were on the move someplace, I don't even remember from where to where, but we saw he was in a lot of trouble. We went and got our mule, came back to his car and pulled him out. That is the way I remember it, but don't put me on a stand under oath because I lost a lot of history from then. We freed him, but he didn't go on to our house to try and make a sale. He told us he would put us on the mailing list for a once a month farm paper for free because he got his car out of a bog. Guess what? We are still waiting for that paper.

We once had a game. We had someone or two or whatever on each side of the house. Someone with a ball threw it over the house, and it had to touch the roof. So no one could throw the ball too far. I think the one with the ball would say something like "Red Rover, Red Rover, let the ball come over," then call a name of the one to catch it, and try to get around on the other side without getting caught. If the catcher got caught, he or she would have to go back. Two or more can play.

We didn't have a bathroom, as we think of today. Our baths took place either out doors or behind the stove in the kitchen, and in the summer we sometimes did it in a tub. When in the house, it was a wash pan. We took many baths behind the stove where it was warm back there.

I wet the bed at nights until I was fourteen years old because of my kidneys. I don't know if they were good because they worked over time to keep me drained clean, or they were bad because they wouldn't sleep when the rest of me was asleep. Alma Lee and I slept together for a few years and J.P. slept in bed with Mom and Dad. Then one day Mama and Daddy thought it time for J.P. and I to sleep together, and I wondered why? Did they want J.P. to get out of their bed? Did they want to give Alma Lee a chance to have a bed of her own? Or was it J.P.'s time to get peed on? I thought I broke a record until I heard of an eighteen year old girl who was at a party and got sleepy. She then went into a bedroom at the party and lay across the bed. When asleep, she wet their bed. That made me proud of myself. Wetting the bed was very embarrassing, uncomfortable, and unnecessary.

We are talking about the days of the Victrola record player. We had one, as did lots of other people. A family came to our house and the radio was being introduced. We had one, but the family visitors didn't know anything about them. They had a son the age between my age and J.P.'s, and we played the radio for the boy. He liked the song the radio played, and he wanted us to replay that song. We tried to tell him we couldn't replay a radio like it was a Victrola, but I don't know if he ever believed us. Back then if you had a radio you had a lot of company, especially on Saturday nights and fight nights when they had boxing on.

When we lived where J.P. met the brick coming off the barn, we had a family living a short way from us, and they had a boy my age. He would go over to our house and play with us. When we got tired of him, we would run him off by throwing rocks from the road at him. Back then most of us wore holes in our clothes, and he had a hole in the seat of his overalls. At one point Alma Lee said "I hit him where the hole is. It went right in that hole." Now that was good. The boy was running, we were running, and she still laid that rock in that hole. At the time it was funny, but he got home and told his mother, and his mother told our mother. Our mother didn't think that was funny, and when she got us we didn't think it was funny anymore. We never used a target with a hole in it after that.

J.P. was always good at shooting a BB gun. I never was any good, but like to pick an argument out of him just to agitate him. He said he could hit most of what I told him he couldn't hit. Finally, I said, "You can't even shoot between your toes without hitting them!" He said he could, and I asked to let me see. We were in a road that led to the mailbox from the lane at our house, so he stood in a well packed rut where the wagon, car, cows and boys kept it hard. He placed the gun well between his toes and pulled the trigger. He thought he aimed at China, but the BB headed for the moon when it hit that hard dirt and then bounced back up. He had two toes with blood blisters.

Everyone knows about the outhouses. When the Sears catalogs ran out, there were always corncobs. There was a saying that when taking cobs to the outhouse you should take three with you, two red cobs and one white one. When the job was done, red ones came into action first then the white one to check to see if all turned out alright.

I guess about all old-timers have their own stories about the house of rest and many stories have been told. I wonder if any are about the same as mine. Mine is about a sassafras tree behind our outhouse. Mama made sassafras tea once in awhile, teaching us the good that came from the roots from those little trees. She said it helped purify the blood and seems to me we had it more in the springtime, but it always tasted good. I use to wonder why Mom and Daddy didn't cut the one from behind the outhouse down for roots since we enjoyed it so much, but when I asked why didn't we use it they would kind of turn it off without telling why. Now I wonder what would happen if we drink the tea from the roots that fed from the waste beneath the seat of the old house where we spent a lot of our resting time. Sometimes we may have had a little more energy running to get in, but coming out we felt a little more relaxed.

Now back to the corn cob. We know how when the corn matured, the kernel set in a little cell or socket. When the corn didn't mature well, the cell around the outlet would be hard instead of soft like velvet and so comforting, but one swipe across the skin would cause some discomfort and we didn't need that. We didn't have any band-aids back then.

Bob, my son-in-law, told me about a small café close to their Mississippi home near Ellisville which has a zip-lock bag hung near the indoor restroom with three corn cobs in it. The color? You're right.

I remember Grandpa Hodges kind of liked me, and I guess all other kids . . . Well, almost all. He said he wanted to teach me how to build houses when I got a little older. I looked forward to that, but the war changed things.

He showed me how to tell when a hammer was balanced before buying one. The claws of the hammer was curved just so that he put the claw end on a flat place with the handle sticking up and rock it back and forth to see how it would settle down and where the handle would be pointing. If it wasn't balanced, well, you just didn't buy it. Now, they make hammers a little differently, so can it still work?

On cold winter days with no TVs in those days, we had windows around that took the place of a television that we enjoyed so much at times. The best lookout point was in the family room, or what we now call the living room. That was the room with a fireplace in it, although when it was cold and wintry and dreary, the small fireplace couldn't keep the house warm with those high ceilings. Our best view from the house was by the fireplace. If it was looking out at the frost on a cold, still and cloudless morning, we saw it and wished we could stay inside all day. If it was raining a little or raining up a storm, we saw it. We didn't have any rain clothes, but we could see it. If the wind was up and was picking up dust we saw it. No one cared to go out in it. It was something different to view the outside from behind the glass window.

We were like the honeybees when we were working with them. If any of them is going to sting us, she would sting the part of the body she saw move. Whatever moved, we glued our eyes on it, whether it was a leaf or a cow, and we watched it. It had our full attention. We didn't have ice on the ground very often and when we did, it was torture just to look out and see it. When we had to do chores or go out for toilet duty or any reason we had to go out we felt punished, but from our best and favorite window it was entertaining to us to see the things that went on outside.

One of our best shows was watching the chickens walk on the ice. They were not familiar with an icy ground to walk on, and as they walked along they would slip down. If they made a fast move as if to run or anything, they would slip on the ice and that was so funny to us. I guess it was because we saw ourselves in that situation when we had to go out and we sure didn't have any Yankee chickens; that was for sure. To slip on ice could give us a most memorable time in our life if we hit wrong, but those chickens were built close enough to the ground that we were safe to laugh at them. They would slip down, get up, look ahead, turn their head one way, then to the other as if to try and figure out, "What is wrong here?" At the time, I thought the chickens had a funny expression on their face, but looking back I think they always looked like that. I just never looked that much or that closely at the face of a chicken before. I now think of the alligator with its smiles regardless of what situation it is in, and the chicken is very much the same. It was more their reaction at the moment that looked so funny to me.

I can still see those chickens trying to watch each other to see if one would find something to pick up. All the other chickens would try to race to see who could be the one to get whatever it was and get away with it. They would start falling and sliding into each other, looking around as if to say, "What are you laughing about? You don't have it either!" All this time they look ragged as the wind was blowing their feathers out of place. There were no groomed chickens until they got some protection out of the wind.

The birds would be looking for food in the field close to the house. There was corn raised there some years and sometimes a bug, a grain of corn, a grain of sand or something could be found around there, but snow and ice would have food covered up and the birds would soon move on and others would fly in and try their luck. There was a hedge tree, fence and bushes close to our favorite place to look and where the birds had a place to be off the ice. Even though we were around birds every day, we still would watch them. Without the snow and ice the birds acted much the same, but summertime was different. We would be out with all these things. Sometimes the birds and we boys, J.P. and me, were afraid. The birds saw us with our sling shots and were afraid we would shoot them down, and we boys were afraid we would miss them.

The cows would mope around as though they were envious of us being inside the house from the cold wind. We were with them each day, but we would watch them; I guess because they would wiggle. I guess any movement would draw our attention. Sometimes they would slowly walk around and seem to look for anything to eat. They would nibble on fodder left on a corn stalk or maybe when there was a cotton stalk they would nibble on the top end of the stalks or grass that was dead. The wind sometimes would blow down through their body and the hair would stick out from them and shake with the wind. They would lie down and would get close together as to share body heat. No wonder their faces were so long, out in the weather all the time, only the barn for a wind break and shelter.

Even the mule had a long face. She was somewhat like the cows when out in the barnyard, and loose with the cows out in the fields. She seemed to have a little more spirit than the cows. Sometimes she would break and start running as if she needed her blood to be pumped up to heat up her body. Maybe to get her sinus cavities opened up so not to get stuffed up in the head and have a headache. She would stop, look up and around with ears sticking forward, then snort with power behind it. We could see when the warm, moist air, all that cold came together it would turn out fog for a ways out there. As a fan, though, I enjoyed the show that they put on for all of us.

It reminds me of when I would be outside in her face to put the bridle on her, feeding her out of my hand or anything that would put me in front of her close by. When she snorted like that, she would fill my face with water and snot. In summertime if she did it, I would not have a shirt on or handkerchief on me, so it would put me on a spot. I did love to lay my arm as much around her as I could but in a situation like that. Needing to clean all that foreign matter from my face, I couldn't wipe it off on her for different reasons. Hair would not be good to dry it off; it only would smear it worse. Loose hair would stick to it. When she would wallow on the ground, sometimes it would be in the cow lot, then not only there would be dirt, but additive from the cows also. I'm sure at the wrong time it wouldn't taste very good.

When a mule snorts all over your face you will right away know you are on the wrong end of the mule.

Once Alma Lee had invited Gene to the house for one of her home cooked meals which he thought was a good idea. That would put him and Alma Lee close together for more time, and it seemed better than where he was living at the time, with Mr. Hensarling and his wife. It would be such a big change he could enjoy. Of course, the whole family was to eat at the same time, at the same place and the same food, so we all had to put up with each other until the meal was consumed. Daddy lead in prayer and looked around the table at the meal Alma Lee had prepared. He saw the vegetables and whatever else that was available, and thought he would start with his usual cornbread and peas. He reached over to break off a piece of bread and put it on his plate with the peas. Now, back then we only put one thing on our plate at a time, and the daddy went first. After we ate that, then we got our next plate of something else; if there were other things set out to eat. Everyone was at their best; after all, Gene was thought of as maybe becoming the next new member of the family. As Daddy broke off a piece of the bread, all eyes were on him. Why? Well, he had broken apart Alma Lee's cake that was to finish our meal, not to start the meal. I don't remember Alma Lee saying anything, but we could almost hear her eyes saying something in a foreign language. All were quiet for a moment.

Once after we had all gotten older, Mama reminded me how I made some people uncomfortable when Gene came to visit Alma Lee. I tried to tell her that it must have been someone else, but she wouldn't buy that. I still tried to hold my own. She said things were going normal until I started out the front door when a rooster was chasing a hen, and I held the door open so all could see it, even Alma Lee and Gene. I thought to be sure that everyone should have enjoyed the show. I later saw Alma Lee and told her of Mama's bad dream. Alma Lee told me she didn't remember that either. I wonder if anyone else remembers that. They are all dead now except J.P. and me. You know he wouldn't tell that story.

Sometimes Mama would get tired of whipping us so she would change the punishment for being naughty. This time she would give us Ex-lax pills or something that we didn't like. One day, J.P. asked me if I swallowed the pills, and I said I didn't know how to get out of it. I asked if he swallowed his and he said no. I said I wanted to know how he got out of it. He said he held the pill under his tongue. The next time we had pills, I made like I put it in my mouth but kept it in my hand. The pills were four cold tablets and very bitter. Later I asked J.P. if he swallowed his and he said he did. He asked if I did and I said no. He said they were so bitter he couldn't hold them any longer so he swallowed his. Then I told him I kept mine in my hand. Many years later, I told Mama the story and she said she did the same thing when her mother gave her some for being naughty.

Another time, Mama put me in the kitchen closet when I was mischievous. That was the darkest place I had ever been in. She shut the door and the first thing I did was feel around the floor, around the jars, and other things that would be there to sit on. I didn't know about the strong smelling, rank, over-aged hog lard in a five gallon container until I ran my hand down into that sluggish stuff that should have been thrown away long before. I had nothing to clean up with or a place to sit until Mama came and let me out on probation. A lesson well learned.

J.P. and I went to Grandma and Grandpa's house when they had a house across the field from us. Mama was there, and like ladies did, was baking cakes and I don't remember what else with Grandma. I was always agitating J.P., which I was good at. When he had enough he grabbed a fork and threw it at me with my short pants. The fork hit the calf of my right leg, prong first and two of the prongs went under the skin, following the skin up to about halfway. Now, here the fork was sticking out and I went in and told Mama to look at what J.P. did, as kids usually do even though there was not pain. Mama hardly looked around and said, "You kids get out of here. We're busy!" I did go out and had to pull it out myself. I don't know if she ever knew or not.

One of our neighbor boys came to our house to be close to someone I guess, and he was out playing by himself with a rod or something and he came by one of our pecan trees. Mama had ordered it years before and had taken good care of it. The tree was a fairly large tree. Mama had dug holes around it so we could empty the hole under the outdoor toilet and put the sludge into the holes she prepared so to use the sludge for fertilize for the tree. Our soil had red clay under the topsoil so it took some time for the water to run through it, so the toilet needed cleaning once in a while. Our friend started to hit the prize tree that Mama had taken so good a care of for a few years. I guess he was just rapping on anything he walked by, for whatever reason we boys did anything. I'm just guessing, but I believe when he saw the bark began to slip off he must have thought it was neat so kept beating the tree. Mama must have wondered what the noise was and went around checking things out and to see what was going on. She got mad and told him to go to his own home and not come back until he learned to take care of other people's property. He ran and would stay just far enough to keep out of Mama's way.

People have ants in their homes, in the yard and most all the places ants can get to where they can either get food or comfort. Maybe people poison them or spend too much to have exterminators to go over and destroy some of nature's handwork. As I see things now, as an old man, things were created for a purpose and nature has a way to keep a balance for living things. When each creature gets too overly populated, there is something else that will destroy enough of that particular creature to balance out nature where there will be food for all to survive hunger, until nature gets out of control and some things become extinct.

I can remember back when J.P. and I were boys looking out for some exciting things to do. At times, we found enjoyment in catching a worm, grasshopper or some bug, throwing it into a bed of ants, and watching the activity as if it was in an arena and we were the spectators watching some kind of sport going on. The creature we threw in would be attacked by the ants from all directions who seemed to be very excited while the poor critter would twist, turn, jerk and roll to try to escape from the hurts and burning of the stings that was forced on it by the ants, until the bed would take the poor thing down into their hide-a-way for food.

J.P. and I were instigating torture, having pleasure in all of that. Some of these kinds of creatures were used as fish bait. I know the hook that ran down the inside of those things caused a lot of pain also, but that was different. If we caught a fish, we were getting food to eat. Either way, we were having fun.

J.P. and I would be out walking around most any place where the cows were. If we saw a fresh pile of cow patty, one of us would run and jump on it with one foot to see how far we could make it spatter while trying to keep the other foot clean. That way we wouldn't have to wash but one foot, as long as we didn't get it messed up.

Whenever Alma Lee would have a friend go home with her and cows would be on the trail where we got off the school bus on the way to our house, if a cow had left a joy pile, fresh and waiting, Alma Lee would try to get us to show her friend what we could do with that cow patty. We wondered, now, if she is so interested in a show for her friend, why doesn't she show her how much fun it could be, but we could never talk her into showing off. We really didn't mind too much showing how it was done though.

Remembering back at the time of my youth and the games we played, I sometimes wonder if the youth today take to playing the games we played. Like jumping rope when two people hold each end and swing it over around and around while one or more people would wait until the moment when the rope was above head high to run in. Then every time it swung on the down stroke, these people that were to jump did that just in time to keep from having the rope hit them on the feet or legs. When they either got tired or missed a jump, they changed places with the two that were swinging the rope. To us, it was fun and joy.

Another, an inside the house fun, was to spin the bottle when everyone was in a circle. As it finished spinning around on the floor, wherever the mouth was pointing, if it was a boy and the spinner was a girl, they had to kiss.

Dropping the handkerchief was another game to play in a circle. One stays inside the circle, another outside, walking around and until they picked someone to drop the handkerchief behind. That one would try to get it before the one inside the circle got it. If not, they changed places. If he did get it, he tried to outrun the dropper of the handkerchief to the spot that was left vacated. Otherwise the two had to change places.

Jumping board was fun, a version of seesaw, or sometimes called a teeter-totter. However, the jumping board was only maybe ten inches off the ground, and instead of sitting on each end of the board like seesaw, the two people would stand on each end and jump up and down. When one would jump, the person on the other end would go up and then, in turn, would jump.

Sometimes we would take two cans, run a string through each of the cans, and tie the strings to leave a hand hold on the center. We would walk with our feet on the cans, lift our feet up by the string as we walked along kind of like we walked with Tom Walkers, a pole with a block up a couple of feet, nailed to it for our feet to stand upon the poles.

I wonder if the kids still do these things as we did. I am not around kids enough to know what they do in their fun times around the house.

One year Daddy grew a large patch of cabbage, and it was a good year for this crop. After they had matured, a man came out, looked at what was in the field, and gave Daddy a price for all of it. The deal was made, and he gave Daddy the money and was gone. We were waiting for him to return, but as time went on I asked Daddy if

J.P. and I could go out into the field and eat some, since the man had not come back. We knew the cabbage wasn't going to be good much longer because we could walk out close to the cabbage and could hear the heads bursting. Yet Daddy told me that he had sold the cabbage and they no longer were ours. It was a challenge for us to keep out of them because we liked to eat the heart out. That was the best part. We were not allowed to even cook them to eat to save a little waste, and being kids, we just couldn't understand. It would be hard for anyone to believe a person can really hear a head of cabbage burst unless they were as country enough to be in a field of cabbage when the action took place.

I remember a day, it was cold and wet so we were inside by the fire to keep warm, and there was a knock on the door. Everyone was looking at each other wondering who that could be. We are way out in the country and only a few people would knock on our door anytime, much less on such a bad day. Most of our kin people would have just walked in. Daddy got up and opened the door, and there stood a black man looking as if he was about to freeze. All eyes were on him and my daddy. We were still wondering who this man was, for I didn't think I had ever seen him before. I heard my daddy say, "Come on in John, and get by the fire. It's cold out there." John walked in, and Daddy got him a chair by the fire where he could thaw out. Now remember, back then when a black person went to see a white family, they would go to the back door, not to the front door. They never went to the front door, but he did and Daddy opened the door and let him in that way. To a child that was very strange. Now why? The man came on in to the fire. He and Daddy had a good visit, and as I remember, he and

Daddy were close to the same age. How did my Daddy know him well enough to call him by name? We kids were quiet and just listened with a lot of questions on our minds. The man told Daddy where he was headed and he was so cold, he needed to warm up before he got on the trail to the road to finish his trip.

After he left to his destination, I asked Daddy, "Where does Old John live?" Daddy said, "Don't ever call a black adult by his first name. Always call them uncle or aunt." He never did tell me where Old John lived. I am glad that the K.K.K. didn't know that Old John went into our house through the front door and out that same door. Years later, I started thinking about that and realized I never was taught at our home to be biased towards black people.

We washed our clothes the old fashioned way. We had a wash pot, built fire under it, and we would have something like a stump, thrown away cabinet, bench or anything that was flat to put the clothes on. We had something made like boat paddles to beat the clothes with when we pulled them out of the hot water in the wash pot. If we needed to rub some of the dirt out, we had the rub board. That was usually a Saturday job. We didn't have very many clothes, but it was a lot of work to wash and it took a lot of time. Maybe we usually did the wash on Saturday because that wasn't a school day. After the wash was dry, then it was time for the starch and the iron that was heated by the wood stove in the kitchen. When the washing machine came out and Mama and Daddy got enough money, they bought one. When it came in, Mama showed us kids how the agitator worked. It seemed to be so slow, and I told Mama I didn't believe it would work. Guess what? I was wrong again. When we got our washing machine, we had just received electricity. That may have been bad to work it by hand. I don't know how we could afford to pay the electrical bill because we were already working with a micro-budget.

We had a pretty hedge growing all the way across the front where the yard fence was and down the south of the yard up to where the smokehouse was in the back. Two mulberry trees were in line of the fence but not with the hedge. We walked out of the house straight for maybe thirty feet or more, and there was the gate to lead through the hedge. The fence was a picket fence with a picket gate to leave the house, or come in the yard, whichever. We kept the hedge cut and squared off real pretty, and it stayed high enough to hide the fence. Well, Mama kept it cut until us kids got old enough to get in a chair and learned to keep it straight. The job wasn't as much fun as we thought it would be and regardless what we or Mama thought, that row of hedges looked like maybe a five year old kid tried to cut someone's hair, but Mama didn't complain too much. Maybe she was glad we finally got old enough for her to volunteer Alma Lee and me for the job. J.P. came a little later as I remember. The fun turned into work after a few minutes, but we had company.

The wasps also thought the hedge was pretty and built their nursery down inside that hide-a-way. We could not find them until they wanted us to see them. Alma Lee and I were afraid we could not be fast enough runners to out run them, and sometimes we were right. We tried to talk to Mama about the situation, but all she would say was to trim around where they were. Now, I just said we didn't know where they were until we saw them, and when we did see them was when they were ready for us to see them and that was when we were very close by without a good running start. I think Mama wanted us to try and spray with Gulf spray we used for mosquitoes, if we had that stuff yet, but she didn't want us to use fire. We learned to run alongside the hedge row and drag our hand across the limbs. If they were in, they usually came out, and we would know how safe it would be. But remember, the wasps were ladies and they always outsmart us males. When they out guessed us, we would be on the run again. Now if it was happening now, we would be after those wasps with a water hose, but I don't know if they made them back then. And if they did, it would be no use to try to sell one to the country people because if there was a fitting to hook one up to a well bucket, it would be hard to get the water to be under enough pressure to knock down the wasps after drawing water out of the well.

One evening, J.P. and I were out playing around with a BB gun, and as I remember, I put a target on the picket gate in between the hedge that we just could see on the other side. So J.P. was getting ready to shoot the target, which he was so good at, and always outshot me anytime. He took his time and slowly pulled the trigger and the thump sounded. Daddy walked up to the gate, met the shot head on, and was hit on the cheek bone. The blood wasn't locked up anymore and freely ran out. He came through the gate way fussing and I don't remember what was said, but he went on in the house where Mama was. She didn't spend too much of her time just standing there looking at Daddy, asking what had he been into, but got busy getting the blood to slow down. I remember them talking about if that shot had been a little lower, there would be no bone there and it probably would have gone all the way through his mouth. J.P. felt bad for giving

Daddy a BB to chew on, and I felt bad because I was in the middle of it by setting up the target. Now, I wonder what the first thing Daddy thought was. That experience stopped us from having a lot of fun. A few years later, Daddy got rid of the hedge and I had mixed feelings about not being able to keep the stuff and yet didn't want to keep it up myself. It was like when I go get a flu shot and glad I did, but missed the flu.

We were short of chairs, so Daddy built a bench and used it behind the dinner table against the wall. Alma Lee and I sat behind the table on the bench looking across at Mama and Daddy which made it convenient to see if we ate as we were taught. We were to put one thing on our plate at a time. We ate that, then, if there were anything else, we got something else, and ate that before anything else was put on the plate, etc. The sweeter the food was the farther to the last it was on our plate. We were to not slouch, but to sit with good posture. One day, I saw Alma Lee whisper to Daddy and I watched her as she sat very properly with a smile on her face, glancing over at Daddy and Daddy smiling back.

Alma Lee asked Daddy, "Who is sitting the straightest now, Daddy?"

Daddy said, "You are."

Mama said, "Marvin is as straight as this fork."

Daddy said, "Yes, but this knife is straighter than that fork."

Mama responded, "Nobody can sit down and be as straight as a knife. If someone is sitting very properly, they will be shaped more like this fork than like that knife."

Daddy gave up. Who can out talk a woman and get along? That was all in fun and we had plenty of fun in our family. Every day wasn't the dark days.

Mama sometimes would correct us at the table for something we needed correction for. This particular time it was J.P.'s day to be led down the path of Mama's rules, and he got scolded for some problem he had. Being very young at the time, he got down on the floor under the table and sulked. We had a small dog at the time and that bothered Mama; a dog in the house with no screen doors and in the heat of summer, but she kind of put up with it. She felt what she thought was the dog and kicked it to make it get out of the house, but it wasn't the dog. It was J.P. that took the kicking, but he never sulked under the table again.

All of us felt sorry for J.P. being kicked like a dog. Mama seemed to be very embarrassed mistaking him for the dog, and J.P. felt bad because Mama kicked him. That wasn't one of our better times until the lapse of time, when we could look back and be able to laugh about it all.

Uncle Leon Hodges would get tired of going out to sea with the Merchant Marines, and would come home to get a job where he could be with family. He went to New Orleans and got a job delivering fish for some company to wherever they needed a delivery made. So he bought a new eight cylinder Ford pickup truck and built a bed that was good for packing fish in ice and going from place to place. He thought it was time to build a house for the family. Time wasn't on his side. He was driving through Carterville and one of the homes had a lot of company because of a holiday. Lots of cars were parked on the street and a boy, I think he was about six years old, started to run across the street, went between two automobiles without looking either way, and ran right in front of Uncle Leon. The finished product was a dead six year old child in the street. It must have been a very long wait for him to stay and wait for the police to get out there, with the boy lying in the street, with family milling around crying and going on. One uncle was trying to say it was his fault and not the boy's fault. The father tried to get the uncle to listen to him when he said it was the boy that should have looked before he ran into the street. Finally, the police got there and after investigating the situation, told Uncle Leon to go on to where he was going.

It was hard for my uncle to get the problem out of his mind. He would go to bed at night and couldn't sleep. He would try to do things at home or anyplace else or do anything else and he would still see the boy in his mind. Finally, he thought the only thing for him to do was go back out to sea. He sold the truck to Daddy so he could leave money to care for his wife and two kids. He left behind a family, but kept a bad memory and went to sea.

One night Grandpa Hodges came to our house to get the truck and told Daddy that Uncle Leon said he was leaving the truck for him to keep until he got back home. Daddy wouldn't give it to him because he bought the truck. Alma Lee was in the house where she could hear all that was said and got scared because things got really loud with Mama out trying to get them separated. I was hard of hearing, and missed all of that, but later on Alma Lee shared with me what had happened. There, the Ford truck was still causing more trouble than even a mechanic could do anything with. It already killed a young boy, and now it looked as if it would break up a family. Does this truck have a future that will bring any good? I guess we can't blame the truck.

When the family was all in the truck at the same time, it seemed most of the time it was when we were going to the church. I don't know if that was where we had been but it was after dark, the dry cows were out of the lot and would be until morning when the milk cows were turned loose to roam into the hills. Then they would all go together to feed. We were almost home, driving down the lane we called a road leading from the road, with lights on. The animals would get confused when lights shine into their eyes and interfere with their seeing how to walk around because they only see clearly the things between them and the lights. Some of the cows were where we were going and one cow tried to get out of the way but as she turned, she saw something but not clearly. That spooked her, and then she turned quickly into the front of the truck. Of course we hit her and broke her tail. Sometime later Alma Lee was talking about the incident and said she didn't know if we could call that a wreck or not. I said to her, "If that had been you the truck hit and broke your tail you would have called it a wreck." She thought that was funny, and after a few years later, she laughingly reminded me of that.

We had a neighbor that would sometimes ride to church with us and would sit in the cab with Daddy while we kids rode in the back. When it rained, our neighbor still rode in the cab with Daddy while we kids got wet, and that didn't go so well with Mama. She let our Daddy know that in a way that he could not miss a word. She said, "That the truck was ours, and not the neighbors, and he should be getting sick instead of us children." I know it put him in a bad position, because he was always ready to give help to anyone in need. In such times as then, we all should work together anyway in order for all us to make it through the bad days ahead. I won't say Daddy or Mama was right, but if it happened to me as a family man, I would think someone should stay at home until a better day, and we had a lot of better days.

Daddy spent a lot of time looking for work. When the other parts of the world got into war with each other, the USA started picking up and opening up a few jobs for helping England and, I guess, others out. Daddy, having two brothers living on the coast, went to stay with them while looking for work there. He found a job with the United States Engineering Department in a dredge boat yard where the dredge boats and other barges went in to get repairs and supplies.

When the war came on, we had rationing on a lot of things, and gas was one of them. Daddy would sometimes leave the truck with us while he worked down on the coast. I was sixteen and went for my driver's license so I could drive the truck to be of more help at home and be, as they said, the man of the house when he was gone. The price was twenty-five cents, and of course no test to take. Now, that made me feel very good and important. That is until a neighbor lady asked me to take her to town and I did. When my daddy came home and some of us told him I took her shopping in town, he read me the rights act because I didn't ask for gas money to pay for rationed gas. Remember how Mama chewed on him for us kids riding in the back of the pickup while a neighbor rode in front with Daddy to church and stayed dry? I also was raised to give help to someone in need, unless it was help for school papers. Now, I am not the man of the house. How can we turn down anyone that needs help?

One summer, when the crops were done, our parents let J.P. and I go back to the coast with Daddy and spend the week. We realized that Daddy was a little slow driving so we decided to watch to see what his top speed was going to be. Every time he would speed up a little, we would look through the back window at the odometer, since we were in the back riding and he was alone while he drove. We had about ninety miles to go and the roads were good. At the end of the long ride, we found that his top speed any place was thirty six miles an hour.

After I went into the service, Mama and Joan moved to the coast with Daddy, so they used the pickup to drive back and forth to work. There was a low place in the road and when the tide was in, the water would back up into that low part of the road. The more it flooded, the more Daddy would drive through it, and the more he drove into it the more the truck would rust up underneath. The more it rusted, the weaker it got, until the frame broke and Daddy had to get someone to weld up some new iron where the break was. He knew he didn't have much more time with it, though he did keep it until he lost his job after the war and Mama and Daddy moved home. Now that I gave out the life of the old 1937 Ford pickup, I will let that rest for now and talk about something else for a while.

Some people used to have a dog that would give birth, and if the dog was a good hunter, it was easy to give the puppies away. That happened to Daddy at one time with a bird dog. He was a black setter and still young. Daddy didn't do much bird hunting because, with the same shot, we could have a rabbit or squirrel with much more meat on it. So the cost of the shot would make a lot of difference, but he liked the dog. Boys and dogs go along pretty much together anyway, so we boys were on my Daddy's side: we liked the dog too.

Now, the fleas were already invented very many years before that, and we always had our quota of those little pests. So when the young dog showed up at our house, the fleas were waiting for a chance of the menu, and attacked the poor critter. One night, the dog was on the front porch in the pitch dark and was tending to those old fleas he had. When he would scratch, he would come down and his paw would hit the floor. Mama had about all she needed of that, so she told me to take the fire poker and try to hit the dog with it. I couldn't see the dog and thought if I couldn't see him, Mama should not expect me to hit him.

I kind of pitched the poker his way, but what I did do was put all of us in shock. I had hit the dog in the eye with the poker going end way, and one end went into his eye about one inch because that is how far the thing was wet. Mama guided me in the care of the dog until he died several days later. He was paralyzed in his back part of the body and there was nothing we could do to bring him out of it. No one got scolded about it but all of us hurt for the dog. But that is life.

We didn't have all that we would want, but when it came to cleaning teeth, I guess there's always a way. I heard when I was a kid, that the Indians would eat fruit like apples, pears or what may have been some types of meat; but we had something much better. We had salt and baking soda and it did what it was said it would do, clean teeth. I learned later that the soda was good to shine and clean metal, so it was good for teeth, too, I guess. The salt was what we used to preserve our meat from the game we killed.

We had a Ford Coupe, I think that was the one that had a mother-in-law seat in it and it was also called a

Rumble seat sometimes; it depended on who was talking about it. Regardless of who said what, it was the same thing. We kids thought it was smart to ride in the mother-in-law seat because it was a little different, I guess. The seat was behind the cab where our trunk is, in today's automobile. It would close up where it looked like the trunk, and if we wanted to use it, it was made to unfold and the seat appeared for seating two people. In cold weather, it was best to ride inside the cab and a good place to not get wet in the rain. I don't know where it got its name mother-in-law seat, unless wishful thinking on somebody's part.

Back in those days, those Model A's, or whatever it was were the thing. Even though Daddy was driving, he had a hard time keeping up with the steering wheel. They were still better than those mules and wagons, unless of course a fellow was taking his sweetheart home. Then the mule and wagon was best, because the mules knew the way home. Think "Look! No hands!" But the car doesn't know where the ditch is so a fellow would have to keep his hands busy with the steering wheel instead of his friend.

We didn't have to feed the chickens much in the summertime, especially with all the bugs, worms and grasshoppers around. On a farm, the little critters had plenty to eat while people were worrying about what there was to eat. The chickens had the cool of the fresh dirt under the house when that hot sun shone down on us, by scratching the top layer off and kind of spread out like there were little chicks under them. I don't ever remember a hen nest under the house. There might have been eggs in the chicken house, inside the barn or out in the open spaces where the grass was and in a shady place. There was joy in finding a nest the hen hid from predators like us and the dog, whether the eggs were good, bad or a hen sitting on them to hatch little ones. If she was there to hatch little ones, she would talk with a special clucking and we would know for sure there were to be some little fellows coming soon. Now, if the eggs were good and no one on guard over the nest, we felt all was well for breakfast in the next morning. We would be excited if we thought of little ones growing up to be born from inside the eggs, but if they were rotten we sure didn't cry. Alma Lee and I knew what to do with them before J.P. was grown up enough to train for that job. The first time for Alma Lee and me, it was "on the job training" for us. Here is what happened. We found a nest with several eggs inside of it. When we notified Mama, she had to check them out before we took them in the house because she had experienced all this before, so she was to be our teacher. She took one and kind of shook it a little and gave us the bad news. Further proof would be to take one, put it in a pan of water, and then if it floated, well, it was a good thought. We were to wait for the next time.

Mama told us not to break any of them around the house, but go down into the pasture, a far piece from the house so no one would have to smell that stench. Were we supposed to break them? Mama didn't say. On the way for the disposal, we tried to be careful and I think we did a good job. We began to talk about what we should do with them. A tree seemed to be a good place to learn what would happen to give us a good reason to want to do the job sometime again. We got to the place we planned for, started to divide the eggs between us and then we took them from the bucket. I had a good thought as I started drawing my pitching arm back. I was looking over at Alma Lee and she was already doing that same look at me. We stood there with a little smile on our face, and then I had another thought. What if she hit me with that rotten egg she had in her hand and if it really stinks bad as Mama tried to make us believe? Now, I don't want to be on the receiving end of that. We must have been thinking the same thought. We both relaxed our arms and started looking at the tree. The first egg that broke open taught us a lot. For one thing, it taught me not to want to be hit with a bad egg. From that time on we were good friends . . . for a while.

There were a lot of homes on high ground with a spring down in a hollow that ran good clean water. So, if a family had that, but short of money, they could go down with a bucket, bring water from the spring for the cooking, drinking and taking baths without spending money for a well or digging a well themselves. Some did their washing of clothes close to the source of water then bring the clothes up the hill to put on a wire line that was fixed between trees. We were lucky enough to have what we called a bored well, one that would be drilled with a machine. I remember helping dig a well for Grandma and Granddad Hodges. The deeper the well, the cooler it got, and it was in summer too. One would dig and put dirt in a bucket; another would draw it out and dispose of the dirt.

Crawfish, minnows, mosquitoes' larva and frogs lived in the springs, so people who got their water from the spring, had to put up with all that and sometimes a stray snake looking for a meal. How do I know that? My wife, Maxine, and I lived on Maxine's mom and dad's farm in a small house after we were married. We had a spring for water and woods for a toilet for a while, until Mr. Hutson got an outhouse and set it up for us. Oh! What a relief!

Now back to the springs. Some springs had water bugs that were black and flat. We use to find plenty of them in lakes, but there seemed to be more in still water in the edge of rivers or creek streams. We caught some and they have a sweet smell that we kids enjoyed. We kids never wanted to kill them. We called the things mellow bugs, and I never knew what the real name was, and I really don't know why they were called mellow bugs.

There was a family that lived across Tallahala from where our family lived, yet in the same community, by the name of Mr. and Mrs. Runnels. They had a girl that was blind. I think she was born that way, but I don't remember. The rumor had it that some people had a little boy by the name of Herman and in later life he was called Hub. His mother had put out the word that they wanted to get rid of him, and if no one else wanted him, she was going to feed him to the hogs, so the Runnels family took him to raise. He and Mary were close to the same age. Many stories went out to tell about him and things he did through the years, and it seemed he had no fear of anything or anyone. One of the stories that stayed with me was the family had to get their water from a spring across the road. Mary had the chore of carrying some of the water, even though she couldn't see. Hub would watch her and just before she would get to the house with the bucket of water, he would tell her that a bug was in the water, and she would throw away the water and go back for more. She would get almost back and again he would tell her that something was in the water again. That was the story that made me dislike Hub Runnels.

There are people still in the Runnelstown community that can still tell stories of Hub and Blind Mary. The highlight of J.P.'s memory of Hub is that he could crow like a rooster, and do a good job of it.

Chicken pox? Oh yes. I remember having that. I wondered why God let that stuff get to us. I never knew where it came from or where it went. About all I knew was it made us miserable. Misery sure had a grip on us day and night, and there seemed to be nothing to help us get rid of that itch under those little sore bumps on us. We had to let it run its course, and it would go away when it got ready, but in the mean time we were not to scratch the scab off any of those sores because it would leave a bad looking scar. Who wants to be ugly? We tried to keep our fingers off of that stuff, but we just couldn't let our minds forget what it was that tortured us. It was an infectious virus disease that just children caught and there were some fever plus a skin eruption. It just didn't seem fair to have something like that around for jumping on to us kids and grownups were free of it, but the grownups always seem to have all the answers. Mama finally made a remark about some saying that if you have the chicken pox you can go inside a chicken house, let a chicken fly over you, the pox would turn you loose, and you would be free of it. Mama said she didn't believe it, but that was only something people said to get a conversation going. Alma Lee and I started thinking. We slipped out to the chicken house. No chickens were there except those on the nest getting ready to lay eggs. Well, we finally made it happen, even though the chickens didn't want to leave the nest, and sure enough we got well . . . two or three weeks later. Hey, J.P., where were you in all of this? Or were you too small to act a fool like Alma Lee and me? It's a thought.

I guess almost all kids enjoyed a little music and singing occasionally, but we didn't enjoy the same songs the same way. We were individuals, so we couldn't think alike on everything. One thing, we were not the same age. This girl boy thing; girls were not supposed to think like us smart boys. Songs that were popular then were songs like "Beautiful, Beautiful, Brown Eyes" and "He Was My Man but He Did Me Wrong," so on and so forth. Alma Lee picked one song that was, "Oh, Johnny, Oh Johnny, How You Can Love." Well, she wasn't old enough for her hormones to kick in, but I wasn't old enough for girls to mess up my mind when I got close to them yet. I still thought of them as being just old girls and not someone I wanted to share my God given time with. When I became a little older and after a couple of heart-breaks later, I still didn't know much about girls. Alma Lee would start singing that song and I just couldn't stand it. Not only not country singing, it was just "love" singing. I would try to get her to go some other place to do her singing so I wouldn't have to hear that "Johnny, Oh, Johnny" stuff, but now she found out how to torture me and she sure wasn't going to let that slide. I would try to ignore what I was hearing, but when I had my limits I would take off after her. She, being older and larger than me, had longer legs too. Out run me? She did. When she had her fun, she wouldn't sing it anymore for a while. Her running, and me behind her was like a dog chasing a car; if I had caught her I wouldn't know what to do with her. If I hurt her, she would hurt me back and I was smart enough to remember the pains of our past when she forgot that I was smaller than she was. In fact, I believe I was having a big part in her preparing to become a good mother in the years to come.

J.P. and I got into the guitar picking fun and I got pretty good . . . I thought. Man, I could play for any song with only three chords to play with. Now, what were the chords that I used? Were they D, F and G? Oh, I don't remember. Maybe that's why I quit and J.P. kept it up. He learned a bunch of chords and made the old guitar sound good. It kind of sung the songs with him. What few homes we were enjoying ourselves in I think the home owners probably wished they could think of a nice way to tell us to go home so that they could enjoy some good quiet time.

We had a small dog that was said to be a Boston bull and rat terrier. I guess with it being a brown dog with small streaks of white down her body, and I think she also had some white around her face she was called Brownie. We use to pick at her and made her mad by taking a stick when she was on the porch and running that stick down across the board that made a lot of racket which she didn't like. I don't remember J.P. ever getting bit, but I would and it was all in the timing. If we stopped at the right time she would let us go without punishment, but I just didn't have it, so then I would cry for a while and then we would go back to doing it again. Boys and dogs just seem to go together very well. One day the dog had a fit, which she had done before, but this time she ran off and wouldn't come back so we felt bad. Mama said that sometimes when a dog starts to die they would leave home to do it, so we thought she must have died. Several days later, she came back and it seemed to make her happy, as it did J.P. and me. She stayed around part of the day, had another fit and the last that we saw her she was running down a row down through the field. From there, she was all history. Back then people said dogs had worms when they had fits, and other people said if someone gave a dog a penny to swallow, that would cure him. The copper in the penny was what some said that got the dog well by killing the worms.

We had another dog which also had fits. When he had one, he would chase one of us into the house or anyplace that kept him off of us. We were all afraid of anything that chased us like he did. Daddy and Mama were concerned enough that Daddy decided he would have to shoot the dog. We had been some place in the car and when we got home, we all stayed in the car except Daddy, and he got his gun out of the house. I could tell he didn't want to hurt the dog and I don't believe Mama did either, but as he raised the gun to his shoulder, there were three of us kids watching a very sad situation that would be in our memories for a long time. Daddy pulled the trigger. A good pet died because he was sick, just moments after wagging his tail, seeing we were home at last.

When doing the chores, it was my job to see that we had wood and kindling to start fires with the first thing each morning, which Mama usually did when she got up before the rest of us got up. We got up after some of the chill in the air was gone but sometimes I, for some reason, wouldn't keep up my share of the chores. Mama would wake me up and have me to go out on the frost to do what I should have done the evening before: get some wood and kindling in and start a fire in the fireplace and the stove. Then I would run and jump back in bed to get warm before I just had to get out of bed again.

Mama would go back to bed after she had me awake to get the fire started, but after the fires were going, she was first to get out from those warm covers and start cooking for the rest of us. Uncle Sam called me into service before I learned to not forget.

Sometimes I sit, enjoying a good cup of coffee and think of how coffee as a brew got its start and wonder how it would be to live back in those days. It goes like this: an old sheep herder was out with his sheep one day when he noticed his sheep playing around kind of high spirited and he began watching and wondering what was going on. Observing his sheep, he noticed them eating these berries that had put on each year at that time of year and kept watch to see if he was really seeing what was making the difference, and then realized that was what made the sheep so playful. From that, people began using coffee beans for a medicine and soon started making a soup with the berries, then sometime later tried them in a brew. It went over big.

When we kids came along, my Mama wouldn't let us drink coffee. She said it was because coffee was the reason she was so nervous, and she wanted to protect us from following her footsteps in being so nervous. We didn't like the taste but always liked to mimic the older people. I could never figure out why older people drank coffee but it wasn't good for kids. It was like cucumbers, we couldn't eat much before they were pickled and couldn't eat much after they were pickled because they would hurt our stomachs. Why raise them anyway or pickle the things when they are harvested? Coffee didn't taste good so why would people drink the stuff? Mama said she drank coffee as a small girl and was hooked on it so that is why she drank the stuff. Because of that I didn't start drinking it until I was married.

As a child, I remember people usually didn't drink coffee but one time each day and that was for breakfast, except for Grandma Hodges. Now she would have a pot brewing in the morning and drink it after it was made way up in the day when the oil would rise up and float on top of the coffee. I wondered how long she was going to live. She lived to the ripe old age of eighty six years old, I think. Those days the cup they drank from was much smaller than today.

I was in the hospital after a gas explosion burned my eyes pretty bad, and there was a man in the next bed to me who said he was from Louisiana and the conversation got into drinking coffee. He said he didn't know why people from that state made their coffee so strong unless it was because during the depression they didn't have enough money to buy the stuff, so they would go out and pick wild coffee beans so they wouldn't have to do without. They adapted to strong coffee so even as the economy got better they continued to drink strong coffee.

To make coffee back then, you would pour coffee grounds in the pot, heat water to boiling and pour the hot water in on the coffee and wait a few minutes, then take out the brew from the grounds and enjoy it. If you were fishing all night you would make coffee in a syrup bucket. I guess coffee must give a person a running start in the morning to be able to hit the day's activity on the run.

Remember the old Sears and Roebuck catalog? Everyone's house got one each year. When someone didn't have an outhouse, I'm not sure what they did to the catalog unless they carried it with them each trip to the trees. That is what we did when Maxine and I were married at one point, until we got our own outhouse.

Without an outhouse, winters were rough. In the summer time, with an outhouse, the wasps were rough.

All the good times we had and people said we were in a depression. A depression? Mama and Daddy did all the worrying for us kids until whipping time, and Mama enjoyed that for all of us.

My School, My Teacher, My Stupidity

One morning, early in my class, my teacher had the class at attention. I was sitting on the front row, trying to hear, but all I could do was see her mouth move. I had hearing problems most of my life, so I learned to ignore what I couldn't hear. When she ran down and was at the end of her speech, I heard her say, "If any of you do, I'm going to punish you." Not knowing what she said, I thought I would be a very nice kid all day, but I made a mistake because I had a wad of paper in my hand that I wanted to put in the trash can, just a few feet from me. As soon as she stopped talking, I got up and put the paper in the trash can to keep my place neat for her.

She said, "Didn't you hear me? I said for no one to get out of your chair without permission!"

Uh-oh! I had done it again!

That, I think, was third grade. When I was in the fifth grade, the same teacher taught me again. That's when she learned I was hard of hearing caused from earaches. We had some sort of work to turn in. She had asked us for types of problems we had that affected us in some way, and I wrote down about my hearing problem. When she read it, she questioned me. John D. Hinton spoke up and told the teacher that I couldn't hear all that was said to me, and the teacher looked so shocked. I wish to have known what she was thinking because she didn't seem to believe me, but when John D. spoke up, it became real to her. If she had known, I may have had more help from her before, but I didn't know how to express myself or ask questions or ask for help.

Once, this same teacher was asking how to spell ache, and I didn't know and failed to spell it. She told me how many times she wanted me to write it down: A-C-H-E. I started writing it down and before I finished writing it all down, the time had ran into recess. By the time I was finished, there was another teacher in the room talking to my teacher.

I handed her my paper, then she said, "O.K., spell it." I did. She said, "Now, what does that spell?"

I said, "I don't know."

She and the other teacher looked at each other and said nothing, but were disgusted with me. She let me finish recess with the other kids, and never mentioned it again.

Three of us boys were chewing tobacco in class, and we kept going to the window to spit. I don't know how the teacher knew we were chewing, but I think it was because she noticed us going to the window too much. She called on one of the other boys to get up and answer some question. To keep from telling her he was doing a no-no, he swallowed the chewing tobacco and got sick. Then she knew for sure and still said nothing about it, but gave us that look that teachers give sometimes. That stopped the chewing tobacco.

The bitter weeds got high and bloomed really well around the school. Power mowers probably weren't thought of at the time, even though someone could mow the weeds with a hay mower sometimes. Well, we boys were told to volunteer for pulling those weeds, and I wished I was a girl so I could play instead. When we were through, I had blisters on top of blisters with all of them busted. When I got home I had a hard time holding anything with my hands and I still had chores to do. When my mama saw that, she exploded. My hands smelled like bitter weeds for several days, and I couldn't even wash them very well. I don't know what my mama said to the teacher or anyone else, but I never had to pull any more bitter weeds after that! Never!

I will tell this story as I remember and think it is correct. At school we had an outhouse for boys and for girls. As I remember, they had two seats in each one, but it may have been three seats. When the W.P.A. (Work Projects Administration) was formed by President Roosevelt, they came one day and started to build two good outhouses with five seats in each for boys and girls.

Sometime later, after they were built, a man went into the boys' outhouse and as I went in, he hopped off the seat to put his clothes back on. His underwear, or as we called them "shorts", were old and he tore them. He looked at me and said, "I don't think I need these anymore," and smiled as he took them off and threw them into the outhouse hole. He was well dressed, and I wondered if people with those kinds of clothes all wore underwear in summer.

I learned something that day. I thought people only wore underwear in the winter, and then it would be long johns. Why do people wear underclothes in the summer? Remember, it was during the depression.

In the wintertime, we planted vegetables that could grow in the cold weather. When any of them were ready to harvest and we could get a sale on them we cut school until we couldn't sell anymore or finished the crop. We may have been out of school for two weeks at a time. It was hard to be out of school that long and catch up on grades. When I was in school, I wanted out. When I was home working, I wanted out. I never knew which I liked better; to learn or to live. We were survivors and money was hard to get.

Sometimes we would get down on the floor by the fire place, where it was warm in cold weather, to get our lessons up for school. Daddy would go into the room and see us by the fire and fuss, telling us to get up to the lamp because we would ruin our eyes because the light wasn't bright enough for our eyes. We wondered about the light a kerosene lamp would put out. Even that kind of lamp we had to get very close to just to be able to see to read.

When we had cold weather outside, we had cold air coming in around the windows and cracks. The ceilings back then were eleven feet high which was good for summer because heat goes up, but when winter comes heat still goes up and fireplaces didn't always keep us warm.

Once we had a test, and after we finished with it we were given a chance to grade our own test papers. The teacher would give us the answer to each question, and we would check it out and mark it right or wrong.

When I got through with mine, I got a very bad grade so I checked right on some that were checked wrong, and scribbled on the ones I lied about. But the teacher pulled a surprise on us and came around to pick up the papers we had graded. When she checked my paper, I had also failed on my scribbling and the teacher asked about my deed. She let me know she was so disappointed in me. As I remember I never cheated again. I think maybe that God and the devil were fighting for me on some of those days.

There were kids in school, and their moms and dads couldn't afford to buy school supplies. Neither could my parents, but they got those supplies some way. Someone was constantly asking for mostly paper and I just couldn't refuse to give it to them, even though Mama told us, "Don't give it away. We can't afford to buy that much stuff." Some of the teachers gave of their own money to help some of their students. In fact, during the depression people helped people in all walks of life.

Coca-Cola Company would sometimes go by the schools and give us cedar pencils, rulers and other little things. Somebody would have a piece of quince in their pocket and some of us who didn't have a quince tree would give our coca-cola pencil for that piece of quince. My mama wouldn't know about that, either. We didn't think of dirty hands or dirty pockets. A piece of quince was truly a delicacy to us kids.

Times were hard and the government was giving out help for some who needed help. They were going to go to our school to give free lunches. Our name was included to receive lunches, so Mama said we wouldn't pack our lunches. The day passed and no school lunch. Mama wasn't happy but was told not to pack one the next day, and that all was alright. The same thing happened the next day. Mama was mad. The third day, it happened the same as days one and two. She started fixing lunches again and I never found out what took place between Mama and the people in control.

I spent a night with Grandma and Grandpa Hodges one night, and the next morning Grandma fixed me a lunch and off to school I went. At lunchtime, we all went for our lunches and after we finished eating the teacher announced that someone got the wrong lunch, but no one spoke up. She asked the little girl if she would eat the one that was left, but she didn't want it. The teacher reported that the missing lunch had mustard spread on bread and the lunch left was a jelly sandwich. Well, I didn't know what Grandma made my sandwich with, and I did eat a mustard sandwich, but I was so embarrassed I was ashamed to speak out. I never knew for sure if I had the right lunch or not.

Sometimes we had fried sweet potatoes for our lunch and this was one of those days. When a potato is sliced, the first slice will have a sharp fringe around the edge and when it is fried, that fringe will be thin and crisp. We, as second graders, would sneak out food from our lunch, not to feed the hunger, but get something by our teacher without her catching us. This day, I got my first slice of potato and as I had a mouthful about to chew down on it, the teacher called on me for something. I don't remember what, but I do remember swallowing the thing to keep from getting caught. With little of it chewed and as I swallowed it, I felt it cutting its way down. I waited for blood, but it never came. That never happened again with fried potatoes.

We kids were taken to a county fair, and I saw a handmade wooden chain hanging in a booth that got my interest. I took one end of the chain and rolled it around to see if I could figure out how it was made. In my mind, I thought I knew the secret and just wanted to be at home in the daylight to try my luck. A few days later, I saw the right sweet gum bush that was soft and just what I could use to try what someone else had accomplished. I cut the bush, cut off limbs that would be in the way, and started to figure out how to enter into a new interest. Waiting to catch the school bus was a good time and place. Each morning as I waited, I worked. I made it work! After a short length of chain made, I found it broken by a bush I had it hid under. After the disappointment wore off, I started again. I had a short length made again and something else happened and I gave up. Fifty five or sixty years later I made it happen. I made two. I did not need the waiting time for any school bus to make a chain. All I needed was a little patience.

Christmas can sometimes be disappointing to a child when the child expects something good and gets nothing, when everyone else gets happiness and excitement in a gift, and you are a child and you think you're the only child that gives and never gets. That happened for a couple of Christmases at school for me, and one year Mama was about as put out as I was. She gave a gift to the teacher to give me, just in case I didn't receive one. We all drew names so somebody was getting something for nothing. That Christmas, like everyone else, I received a present and felt so good. I think it was Alma Lee that told me years later that Mama told her about how Christmas had turned out for me, and she came up with the idea to be sure I had a good Christmas, too.

Our teacher taught us how to make paste the easy and cheap way because money wasn't too plentiful. We made paste with water and flour. It wasn't as good as store bought, but it lasted long enough to paste paper together and get it home.

Once we had a program at school, like we had about once each year, I think, for making money for the school. They had booths and tables set up for games that cost like one cent, two cents, etc. I walked up to one booth, paid my penny (I really think it was five cents, but it has been a long time), was given a fishing pole, my line went out of sight, and then I waited until I felt my line jerk and pulled it up. Surprise! A new type of ink pen! The old type was the kind we would write with, but the ink bottle would have to stay open, and as we wrote we dipped our pen in each time we needed more ink. Now, I had my very own pen that would hold enough ink that I could keep writing without dip, dip, dip. It had a bladder inside of it, but it was used too many times and the bladder would not hold ink. This program was like a flea market where people brought stuff they didn't want, and a busted bladder, nobody wants. That's the story of my life. I was back with my old type ink pen.

The school was also used for other things than the dreadful days of learning to pass a test. I remember we had a man who called himself Zeke, Fiddling Zeke. I guess that's the way you spell his name. He was a one man show, telling a joke now and then to break up his playing routine. As I remember, it cost ten cents to get in to see and hear him. He would play the fiddle a little while and then put the bow between his legs, with the fiddle being behind him he would play a little, then put the fiddle behind his neck and play, then put the fiddle behind his back and play. I don't remember much else except he was good.

One of his jokes was about a man telling a story. "There was a man telling someone about a goat. He said, 'You know that goat didn't have a nose?' The other man said, 'If he didn't have a nose how did he smell?' The first man said, "Awful!" Then he went on with his show. The memory of a child . . .

Some of the communities would have an all night gospel singing in the school, as there was more room to sit people than any church in the area, and they would let one group sing for a while, then another, on and on. The only time Mama and Daddy took me with them, I just knew I could stay awake all night (even though I couldn't keep awake just a couple of hours in night church). The only group of singers I remember was the barber shop quartet. Four of the men made up the quartet and they would be working the barber shop, and when time would permit, they sang together on songs that they would be singing some place they were to go. That was before electric clippers. I wonder when the electric clippers came into being. As a young child I was hoping maybe one day to being a barber shop quartet member, but I never learned to cut hair or sing. Some of us are losers.

The school, as I remember, was as the church, having carbide lamps, not kerosene. Carbide made a much better light and good for a group of people. Oh yes. Did I keep awake all night? You guessed right. No! And those seats were not even as comfortable as church benches.

School was hard for me, and as I said before, work came before school. Also, I didn't know how to ask for help with my lessons. In fact, I don't know yet who would have had the time to help me. We only had eight months of school in the country when city schools had nine months. For the first four weeks and last four weeks, we only had one-half days because if we had school all day, we would have to stay home all day to pick cotton. The spring was planting time plus hoeing-out grass that grew with the crops. With those kinds of problems, I failed the seventh grade. The next school term someone kept telling me to go talk to the principal and he would let me go to the next grade, so I thought what the heck, so I did. He was nice, and said he would, but if I didn't keep my grades up, he would send me back to the seventh grade. So, I thought I had it made because the eighth grade was said to be easy to pass, and I did pass it.

I was small when we had no gymnasium. I do remember when our basketball court was on the west side of the school. In fact, it was so close to the back door facing the teacher's home that someone could sit on the steps leading into the school. Of course, not many people could sit on short steps leading to a single door, but I added that to say it was close to the building. What I remember was we had two courts, one for boys and one for girls. I don't know if we had bleachers, I just don't remember them being there, but I do remember standing to watch the game for a while and moved around to get rest from just standing around to watch. That was something I didn't care much about. I liked to have a good time to run and play with schoolmates.

When President Roosevelt and his people formed the WPA to help our economy get a boost, one thing they did was help some of our schools, and our school really received a first class gymnasium. Before in-house ball games started, when it rained, no ball game. After our gift, it could be some rough weather and we still could play ball as long as the lights didn't go off. As long as people made it early, before the weather got bad, they could watch their favorite team play.

One thing in my memory of those days was the talk around the community that the WPA was short for "We Piddle Around." I really don't think it was, but maybe the men needed a job so bad, they may have sort of worked a little slow so they had a job a little longer, I don't know. WPA was for "Work Projects Administration". The WPA helped some people in some ways, and the C.C.C. helped in other areas like setting out trees and building lakes. Those people got to use clothes like army clothes, and got paid twenty one dollars a month, the same pay I understood, as the National Guards. The Civilian Conservation Corps turned military when World War II started. We, the family, had kin that found himself in the military service; which was unexpected to us at the time. They still had a job for the army, National Guard or somebody. I don't think that happened with the "We Piddle Around" bunch, though. After the WPA was gone, we still had a strange stench in the gym like it may have been from perspiration and something like a chemical mixed. After being in the gym for a while we soon forgot the stink.

I think about the changing from one grade to another. It is like different levels in our education: we grow older, get better advanced in knowledge, prepare for the outside world, and are then able to choose our own future as to which way we go in life. For some reason, I think it was easy for my school elders to be able to choose the ones that should be on the work party and the others that needed a break from working in the classroom. I felt I was popular when work showed up. I saw the levels in the work department something like, picking up paper and trash around the school grounds, and passed to the next level for the work area which we would sweep where needed, mop where it was needed and then on the court, we had bags of fresh pine sawdust to broadcast on the playing area and sweep it up. We would take out the trash, and anything that needed to be done. Hot dog! Now moving up to that level, we are out of the hot sun in summer and cold wind in the winter! How about that?

Now after age permitted, we got on the ball team. Now, that was the place. We needed to practice often to be good and we called it working out. Working out? It was more like playing out. No more working in the school area. Working out was not always learning the feel of the basket ball, but exercising. Like running so many laps, which we were not use to doing before ball season started and our legs sure would get sore for a while. The principal was also our coach, and enjoyed easing up to our back, kicking the sore calves of our poor legs, and making some sarcastic remark without any pity. I guess he was trying to teach us to be tough, but it didn't work on me. The other exercising didn't seem to be so bad on us.

When we got well and got all that out of the way, we were ready for some ball. You may know what it's like to be a boy on a team and people were paying ten cents to go inside and watch you play ball! Well, I never got good at playing ball, but I feel there were a lot of students who have good memories of things, public and private, that no one else would be interested hearing or knowing about it. I wonder if we could have done better if air conditioning was available. My playing basketball never got good, whether temperature was hot or cold, but I enjoyed playing if the other people liked it or not.

I did make first team before I went into the service, but it was because all the older players got drafted before I did. Oh well, the games we played in service were a lot more exciting than basketball was.

One of our women school teachers was large, but not too large, Mrs. Ford. She was a somewhat quiet, but stern lady. One day, she was walking along on campus, talking with another teacher when her underpants fell and almost covered her shoes. She slowly stopped, stooped down and pulled them up away from her feet, wadded them up and walked into the school house without as much as looking around. Just as if she had that happen before and hardly let it stop their conversation. She didn't stay in Runnelstown very long, but that wasn't the cause of her leaving.

Today's mornings before school start off much differently than those childhood days when we lived on a farm. Those were the good old days anyway, we all know. The good old days to not have to go back to! I have wondered about the old people from years before my introduction into this old world on up to my start in life, because we have had so many things people have thought up to help us be lazy, comfortable and forgetful. We don't care much for our neighbors any more as we used to. How were we different? Let us go back into my past and see if I can remember some of the ways my life was, and started into a good, or even a bad day, before we left to go to school. Did we enjoy life then?

Let's start with winter. Mama would wake up to start a fire in the fireplace and the stove. Thermostat? What is a thermostat? Oh! I knew we were a lot of things, but a thermostat? God made us to be a thermostat, huh? Well, I am glad that man finally came up with man's idea for temperature control. If the house was too cold, I would jump back in bed and wait for some heat from the fireplace to warm up the room a little. I say little because with high ceilings and the way the house was made, plus the fireplace was letting a lot of heating go out with the smoke because yesterday's world didn't let us have today's material and ingenuity.

This wasn't always my job, and maybe when I did have to get up first it was because my job at the time was to have plenty of wood and kindling, which were thin wood splinters to get a quick fire going. I was sometimes slack in doing my chores, so if the wood wasn't there, I could sometimes brave Jack Frost and get the wood for starting a fire. This is part of the training to help me to remember what I need to check on the night before bedtime and not after get-up time the next morning. Frost on wood makes fire nervous and it takes its time before the wood would burn. Bed never felt better than it did when the fire burned slow. I remember going back to bed to wait until the house got warm enough to slide into clothes that are to be worn for the day, and then the clothes were still cold.

Next we put on our coat, went to the kitchen and got the milk bucket, put water in it and headed to the barn. We got feed out of the crib so the cow would stand still all the while we were milking, and if there wasn't enough feed to last long enough to finish milking, we had to get a little more. The cow seemed to learn that if she would hurry and eat fast she would get more feed. Sometimes she would not let the milk go down until the calf was put in with her. Then she would let the milk go down. When we saw the bag fill up we pulled the calf off from the cow, and shut the gate on the calf until we got through milking as much as we wanted, leaving some for the calf to grow on.

If the rain came and the lot got too wet, of course we had to bog through all that mess without boots or shoes. We had a well for water, but not a water hose to wash our feet or shoes. We were taking care of the shoes, and why not? We only got shoes once a year.

We would take the milk in the house after putting the calf with the mother. Sometimes I strained the milk and other times Mama would. When J.P. got old enough to milk the cows we did it together.

Alma Lee had plenty to do in the house and never did have to do the milking. When she and Mama got breakfast ready, we would eat, get up and separate the cow from her calf and turn the cows loose to go feed on the open land behind our farm. The calves would be in the field or a patch close by the lot.

When we had hogs, sometimes we had to feed them, but usually that was only at night. The mule needed a few ears of corn to let her know where to go each night and after putting feed in her trough each night we would shut her up until morning. After morning feed, we turned her loose in the patch before going to school.

After all of that, we cleaned ourselves up for school and, at times, we went to the highway and waited for the bus. If the weather was bad, we would go inside a home that was there, until the bus got there, then we would spill out to the bus and run to the school. Later, the bus stop was where the post office changed our mailbox stop to, where the road ran just a few hundred yards from our home, and where the trail ran to. One way it went south to Mack Carter's home and west the other way to where the Travis' home was.

We waited for the school bus each morning unless the weather was too bad. There was no home there to go into to wait for the bus. Now, if we missed the bus we walked to school with hopes to be on time the next day. If the weather was too bad, we would stay home because the bus did not make that short run to our house to keep us dry. For cold or heat, we didn't miss.

After each weekday at school, we went home to do field work or whatever needed to be done around the house, and then undo or redo what it was that we did in the morning. We cut the wood and took it inside the house where it needed to be, fed the mule and shut the stall door behind her, slop the hogs, fed the chickens, fed the cows and milked those that were to be milked as in the morning (the cows not milked wouldn't get food very often in the summer), be sure the cows were shut in and calves shut out. We tried to keep a lick salt block out for the mule and cows, only when we had money coming in. Otherwise, the cows would lick metal, like plows, or anything that tasted salty.

Sometimes, a cow would die and the owner would perform an autopsy on it to see if they can find anything that would make it sick enough to die. Sometimes they would find barbs from barb wire, sometimes some short pieces of wire, nails, and anything that tasted like salt that could be swallowed. So we did like to have salt out for the stock.

We would either get beside the fireplace or next to a kerosene lamp for light to study our lessons, even though Daddy would fuss sometimes when we studied by the fireplace. He would say, "You are going to ruin your eyes down by the fireplace. Get up here by the lamp." Have you ever studied or tried to read using a kerosene lamp? We would eat supper and wash up for bedtime.

The next day it all started again. Saturdays, of course, would be no school, and then there was more time for work and chores.

Sundays, there was no work except chores and church. I wondered when I learned that the Bible said no work on the seventh day, if we were committing sin when we did our chores. After all, chores are work. That didn't help when I brought this up with Mama though.

In The Woods and Fields

Aunt Mary Lee's husband, Uncle Short, butchered a cow down in the pasture for a little money. He left all the guts, blood, and all that stuff not eatable on the ground when he got through. When the cows came in from near the foot of the hills behind our property, they begin to smell around all that mess, then began calling out for the dead. Ralph, J.P. and I went to see what they were talking about, not knowing what had happened. We walked right in with the cows and didn't know they were talking about us. When they begin to break rank and head for us, we headed for the fence and at the same time looked for our tree of victory on the way out, but found none. But J.P. lucked out and found his to climb and get away from those mad cows. Ralph and I got through the fence. Now, the cows were strolling around that tree as if to wait for their prey to come down, so they could reach him. On the other side of the fence were us boys wondering, "How are we going to get J.P. out of that tree?" J.P. was diagnosed at a younger age as having polio and it left him with a bad foot. It was not the worst case of polio, if that was what it was, but his foot was left crooked. When questions arose about how he climbed that tree so fast, someone said the foot was curved to fit the tree. Someone else said that fear was better to climb a tree with than a curved foot. I don't remember how we got him down, but I think when the cows moved out, we must have moved in.

We had nettle weeds growing in the pasture. We were always without shoes in the summer time, so being barefooted, we found lots of things that we would have otherwise missed. When we hit nettle with bare feet, we had stinging feet, but someone told us a remedy. When you get into nettle with bare feet, you stop and pee on the spot where the nettle got to you. No more problems. Isn't that neat?

One of our best times of a past time that we did not do very often, was ride the vines that ran up into the trees and very high up. We didn't do it often because we had to go a little ways from home to get to them, I suppose, but we did that down on the river bottoms and it sure was fun. We would act like we were Tarzan. It wasn't just Bullace vines, but anything that looked like a good ride. We would test it out and see if it would hold us up. If it felt good, we would cut it off someplace close to the ground, and then give it a check out to make sure we would not break our neck before we would ride it through the air. We liked it near a bank of a branch, or any high spot before a lower level, where we could run with speed and jump into space, ride through the air and swing back for another ride. There was something about a live vine to ride on, such as not being a risk at breaking when we were airborne. Usually, if it was going to turn loose from the limbs of a tree with our weight on it, it would do this slipping slowly so that we would have time to end our "riding the vines" before getting hurt. The way the vines would wind through the limbs would cause the vines to turn loose from the tree slowly, giving us plenty of time and keeping us from getting hurt.

Some people used vines to ride over water and drop off, then swim back to the bank for more rides. We didn't have the pleasure where we went swimming. Later, we saw rope tied up in a tree to get the same fun.

Another treat was shooting birds with our sling shots and building a fire to cook our kill. No salt, no hog lard, but we thought it tasted good. We ate well in the woods, in the summer time anyway. Raw crayfish was a little sweet. The things that went through our minds . . . Bullace was good, opossum grapes a little sour but good, persimmons were good after a frost (ask any opossum). Crab apples were sour, but good in the fall and with a pocket full of them we would eat until we saw a bird and then use them for ammunition for our sling shots. We ate different kinds of berries: huckleberries, dewberries, blackberries, gooseberries and strawberries.

The way we caught crayfish was with our bare hands, a seine made from a potato sack or string with a piece of pork on it for bait, like fishing with a cane pole. We also used worms for bait.

We hunted rabbits without a gun. Our dog would chase them into a hollow tree. We would get a limb from a bush or tree and twist a hold on their skin and pull them out. Then we would grab them by the hind legs and sling their head against a tree. Poor rabbits . . .

We had fun catching fish in some of the sloughs in the woods or fields. We took a hoe and rake with us to muddy the water hole and wait for the fish to come up for air, because they couldn't stand all that mud in their water. We would have fish for supper.

Once, J.P. and I heard the dog barking and went to see what he found. Well, it was a skunk and he ran into a gopher hole. We ran home and got a shovel to help the dog out. We three paid a price for that skunk. The dog got sick and we had to go home. When we saw Mama, she got mad. She also had the last word. I wondered how she knew we killed a skunk. We had another chance to serve our Boy Scout tradition by helping someone else. That dog needed help again to make another kill. When we got home Mama met us again. She knew what. I thought she must have been psychic. How else would she know of the skunk? We learned a lesson, never play with a skunk until we can move out on our own. But why didn't she fuss about that civet cat?

A cow trail in a pasture or in the woods, with the help of a good rain, gave us our own water slide. We would see a good spot, backup, take off running on the grass for a good foot hold and hit the trail with both feet sliding with the turns of the trail. That was as good as skating, and a lot cheaper. Besides, we had no place to skate.

Sometimes, we could find what looked like a course hair stretched out a few inches long. I was afraid to pick that up because not knowing what they could do. They were always in a cow trail and wiggled. Talking to a friend, he said his dad or someone told him a mule hair would come alive in the water, if it came out of his tail. Oops! I mean, off a mule's tail. (That makes a whole different story don't it?) I talked to J.P. to see if he remembered that and he said he had pulled hair from the old mules tail and twisted it some way and it would wiggle. Anyway, we sure learned a lot; a lot that was questionable, that is. Shush!

Every year, when we had planting time in the spring, we had a lot of persimmon sprouts to dig up to keep them from getting in our way when we worked the crops. I remember we dug very deep to keep them from coming back up from the roots. I could not figure out how the roots would sprout out new growth. That stuff was like Bermuda grass, we just couldn't get rid of it. I asked J.P. why was it that it kept giving it back to us when we worked so hard to get rid of it. We had persimmon trees around but not close enough to go that far into the field. J.P. said the opossums ate them, and then went out into the field and broadcast the seed since their stomachs couldn't digest them. J.P. is a lot of help with this story and without him helping me I wouldn't write it up. He has a better brain than I do, because I can't remember so well.

Someone, and I think maybe it was the Travis', told Dad he had a young cow hung up in a branch that flowed from the hills behind our home. There were no stock law on cows and we just opened the lot gate, let them out and away they went into open range. Everybody's cows knew where home was and sometimes they would feed on the grass together and group up with their own when they would start to leave the area. The cow got down in the branch and was foundered and died where she was. Dad got Gene. I don't think J.P. was there, so it would be the three of us in the woods, and we would go from one stream to the other looking for the cow. We had walked a long time up and down the hill until I got tired and thirsty. I got where the water was flowing good from springs at the head of the branch, so I could get a good fill of water before climbing up another hill. I finished getting my fill of water and we started up toward the head of the branch when I looked up and saw the lost cow, with all the water running around her. Now, I don't feel so good. Why didn't I go to the head of the springs? Well, we had about given up, is the reason for being so stupid. Another lesson learned. It must have been a good cow, because I never got sick. I know now, you hunt a dead cow starting from the springs and go downstream in case you find her.

One of our cows came home with her skin scratched and the bush of her tail gone. She was tired from running and was in slow motion. I asked Dad what happened to her. He said Hugh Carter tied a can with rocks in it on her tail and sent her home. How did my daddy know all that? Well, as I said, there was no stock law there at that time and sometimes people's fences didn't keep the cows out of the fields, and maybe my daddy knew more than he told me. That is, if he wasn't joking. J.P. and I, as far as I remember, never did that; but there was a chemical that came out we called Hylife, although it had another name. We may have put that on some animal that did not belong around there. I remember a poem that was from a child's book talking about the cow that jumped over the moon, but I believe that was before Hylife was available to the farmers. It was put out to put in cribs of corn to get rid of weevils or such. Do you think that might be what happened to that cow?

I always liked picking cotton, but I never saw a hoe handle that fit my hands. I remember I was fast, and I could out pick Alma Lee. That is until she would start talking to me in a low voice knowing I couldn't hear very well, and I would have to slow down to hear, then she would get ahead and I would have a hard time trying to catch up. She was always out smarting me. As long as we had turnips, mustard, etc., school had to wait.

We share cropped the field on top of the hill behind our house one year and planted cotton. It grew and made good, except at the end of the rows where the woods were, and the cotton grew short there. We called the short cotton stalks bumble bee cotton, where the bee can sit on the ground and suck the top bloom. It was getting toward the end of the day and as I was reaching down to a bowl of cotton I saw a Rattlesnake coiled about ten or twelve inches below my fingers. The first I had ever found and I was afraid to move. Lucky for me, he was sleeping in the shade of the cotton leaves. I eased back, and got a stick, killing it and taking it home with me to show it off to the family. I was really proud of what I did.

On that hill, we hunted and found a lot of arrowheads. I gave most to one of Uncle Burkett's boy in Florida. I use to wish I knew the history behind the arrowheads and the Indians that made them.

When corn and cotton harvest was over, the stalks needed to be gotten rid of. We would pick up corn stalks, pile them up and set fire to them so they would not be in the way when we started plowing. The cotton stalks were more trouble, and Daddy would borrow a stalk cutter and try to plow as much as he could, so as to let them rot. One year, he cut a gum tree down and took out a good looking block from it. I don't know now how long it was, but he had it all figured out, and sawed the block lengthways a few inches deep around it. Neither do I remember how far apart, but maybe four inches, where as it rolled it would cut the stalks in small pieces so to be easy to plow under. He had collected cross cut saw blades and broke them the right length, put them into the saw cut and drove the blades into the notches, a little farther down than the saw cut was deep, so to keep them from falling out. He made the shafts to hitch the mule to it and all was ready. The block was heavy enough to cut the stalks if he waited until they were dry enough to be brittle. The stalks were ready to plow under.

A neighbor, Mr. Byrd, was a good farmer and knew how to raise and produce early like sweet potato slips (some called them sweet potato draws) and put it on the market early, soon after the frost was over. Frost would kill them if too early. It was a mystery to me, until I saw how he did it. In the winter Mr. Byrd went out into the edge of the field where the tree line started, so to use the trees for protection from the strong north wind, and dug a trench, covered it with roofing tin, then covered the roofing tin with the dirt that came from the trench and left each end open, boxed all around the bed with poles. He prepared a shelter made of cotton sheets, like on a bed, where the sheets would be up higher than the potato slips when they came up. On one end of the trench, which is now a tunnel, he fixed for a fire box to warm the soil, using slow burning wood. On the other, he fixed for the exhaust and a way for a damper, like a stove pipe. This is to keep a low fire to warm the bed when he needed it. The sheet also came off on warm days. The timing is very important to put the sweet potatoes in the bed at the right time, and he knew just when the time was right. When the slips were ready, the time was right for the market to want them. He told daddy to come over and get what he needed for his crop. He was a good neighbor, and a friend to us and others of the community.

Mr. Jim Byrd was an expert when it came to fishing and also at making coffee on fishing trips. With no television, and very few radios, the past time back then was telling tales. Someone told one on Mr. Byrd. As I remember, this is kind of how it went. Several of the men around that were regulars in one group were on one of their trips down Leaf River where fishing was fun. One of the men was Slim Pierce who had lost a leg and one eye. He was quiet, seldom smiled or laughed, and was a business-like kind of man that enjoyed life his own way. All the trout lines were in place, baited and waiting for a fish to come by and taste the bait. It was time to eat a bite, for those that may be hungry after working hard to seine bait, getting the boat in the water ready to put out lines, putting up camp and just waiting. Mr. Byrd was the one that always made the coffee. He got his syrup bucket out, filled it up with river water, raked out some hot coals from the camp fire and put the bucket of water on a level place so as not to let it fall over. The night had just come in on them, taking away the day light. They depended on the camp fire and a food can that had been filled with gasoline, hung on a tree, and then lit for light to see by. The coffee is ready for the water to be poured in when it would begin to boil. Soon, the water started to boil, while Mr. Byrd held his eyes on the situation, about the time that all was ready to put everything together. While the steam was coming out of the bucket, a moth came circling around and hit the steam. Down he went right into that hot water. Slim had leaned against the tree close by, as if he was in a lazy boy chair, and had just dropped off into a sleep. His legs were stretched out on the ground. Mr. Byrd took the bucket, slung it out to get rid of the water, so he could start all back over. Just as he slung it toward the bushes, kind of behind himself, he looked and saw that hot water go right across Slim's legs and he ran over, slapping his pants legs to get the hot water off before it had a chance to get through his pants and burn Slim. Slim slept through it all without moving. Mr. Byrd was so surprised that Slim was sleeping so well, until he realized the water went right across only Slim's wooden leg.

Across the Tallahala and a little north of the Old Eddy, are two lakes called The Rubin Lakes and why they are called that, I have no idea. But J.P. and I went to them one particular time to try our luck. The lakes are small but looked unmolested, the limbs reaching several feet over the water, the fallen leaves on bottom that could be seen from the edge of the water, no muddy water in the shallow, very few logs inside the lakes, no particular pathway going in or out except a trail animals may leave or the inlet for the water drainage from higher up and drainage out of the lakes themselves. There was an old boat that was there a long time before in the edge of the one lake. All that was left was a part of the bottom of the boat with the nails still in the boards, sticking straight up, but the leaves that had settled down on the bottom of the boat had almost hid the nails and rust was slowly devouring those nails. We were trying to catch a few fish, and the way the limbs were spreading over the water, we were having some trouble throwing our hooks where we wanted them to go, for nature had overdid it some. J.P. eased slowly out on the boat bottom to throw out his bait and looking where hopefully the fish may be, not where he was walking, he stepped on one of those nails. We both thought we must go, after seeing how bad it was because of how bad the swelling would be before we could get home. He tried to walk but soon found he just couldn't go unless he had some help. I had stepped on enough nails to know how he was hurting and felt so helpless to know I couldn't do anything to help him. We were a long way from home. We decided I would carry him on my back as far as I could then figure out what we would do from there. When we got to the river, I didn't think I could make it. When we got to the logs and I had to walk with him on my back, we had a must. He must walk those logs with me holding on to him. When we got across the river, I had him to crawl back on my back again and away we went across the sand, around the Old Eddy, through the woods, and on to home after a few stops. He hurt bad and didn't want to stop, but we did what we had to do. Once at home, all he needed was a mother's love and a mother's touch and she was waiting. I don't remember now if it was the kerosene or boiled some Red Oak bark she used or both. I believe J.P. may be able to remember what she did, but a mother's love he had plenty of.

I remember when J.P. and I went to the Rubin Lakes with Ralph and no, we didn't catch what we wanted, but the less we catch the less we do have to clean. So, we still had a good time! We thought it was time to go home. We had those logs to cross over on the get across Tallahala and when we got there, we had the fishing equipment we had to take care of and that got in our way at times. Ralph went first with the things he had which didn't keep him from getting out of balance. He missed a step and down he went hitting the water, and I mean under the water. His head was wet, as was the rest of him, and I told him that with the waste from the Masonite Company being in the water, all his hair would be falling out. That had him worried, and he asked us if we were sure, was he going to lose his hair? We had a good laugh out of it but told him I was lying. All was well, but I believe he was wondering if I was really telling the truth. Ralph died in Africa during WWII serving in the Army, and I think he died with all his hair.

Someone told Daddy how to make some extra money and who to contact. The government was planting quail in some other part of our USA and was in the market to buy them. We had the large Bob White Quail that had some meat on them and that is what those people wanted. Mississippi had a law that said people in Mississippi could not kill them legally but the United States didn't have a law to keep people from catching them. Daddy built a cage like when we had a chicken we wanted separated from the rest by placing it in a cage, but this cage had no bottom in it. Daddy then dug a trench as long as he needed, put a board across the trench just far enough for the end to be at least half way inside the cage, and some corn was all on the ground inside. That wasn't talked about around the house for security reasons so I don't know how many he caught or how much money he made, but now I wish I could have remembered to have asked him about that after I was grown.

Some sportsmen's club was cause for the Mexican quail being brought to Mississippi by our government and turned loose. They were smaller and fast, so the sports men wanted fast birds to be more sports like. The farmers that were raising them on their farms wanted meat when they shot a bird, but the city slickers won that one. The quail we had and Mexican quail was put out in order to mix and make a middle size, fast quail.

I was sixteen when the power company came through our community cleaning a right of way to string up electrical power lines for our first electricity. It seemed to me everybody was very happy, but now after all these years I wonder if there were very many people really counting their money to see if they could afford this kind of luxury. The crew was getting close to our home and cutting trees, which were tall pine trees that air could not escape out from under this hot, hot wilderness. A foreman came by our house and asked if I could handle mules enough to drag trees that had been cut to an out of the way place that would allow the crews to put up poles and run wires to go through with their jobs. I told him I thought I could. He said their mule skinner passed out from the heat and they needed the job to move on, so off we went with one half of the day was yet to come. I had been told the men were getting four dollars a day so I expected to get about two dollars for my time. That was big money for those days. The trees were thick, and as they were sawed down they were piled on top of each other. I was climbing over logs to hook the mules to each log, drag it off, come back for the next one, on and on, until close to dark. On to the house we went, and he was going to pay me. He reached in his pocket for change; he counted out forty five cents, handed it to me, and thanked me for helping out. I felt bad that forty five cents was all I would get for a hot job a grown man had problems trying to do and couldn't stay on his feet. As time passed by, I realized I could drive a pair of mules, but I had no experience in the timber. Maybe the foreman was good to me, but try telling that to a sixteen year old!

When WWII started, our president said that we were not getting into the war and getting our people killed, but he did support England and England welcomed people there into their Army. At the time, Franklin Roosevelt was our commander in chief and he allowed men to go and enlist. Grandpa Hodges wanted to help fight in the war and knew he was too old. To make himself look younger, he cut all his hair off to keep the gray hair from showing, went down to the recruiting office to enlist into England's Army and told the man he wanted in. The recruiting officer man asked his age and was told he was sixty years old. The officer told him, "Mr. Hodges, I can't sign you up because of your age." Grandpa said, "I can out-do any man you got." The officer said, "Mr. Hodges, I don't doubt that any, but I have my orders and if I don't abide by their rules they would punish me."

Uncle Leon Hodges was like his father, my grandfather, and he was a merchant marine, going almost all over the world. After Japan started war with us, Grandpa asked Uncle Leon if he would take his knife and kill him a Jap with it. So Uncle Leon said yes and took the knife from Grandpa. Now that knife meant a lot to Grandpa. It was a heavy hawk bill knife that people didn't see much and, as I remember, he thought that it would be easy to cut a man's throat. Uncle Leon was also very patriotic. Once, he was on a ship that went to some of these islands, I think around the Solomon Islands, maybe Guadalcanal. For some reason the ship was anchored for a long time, so Uncle Leon thought he should be helping win the war and not just sit there doing nothing. He went ashore, helping the troops take supplies up to the front lines. One day, he was on a trail, going up front and saw the dead Japanese bodies around on the ground. The Japs used bodies like that to use as a way to fool our people into thinking all the bodies were dead. As a man walked by, he would sit up and attack from behind with a knife to make a killing. Uncle Leon saw there was something different about one of them, and as he had been trained to do, he kept an eye on him. When Uncle Leon saw him move, he got ready for whatever was about to take place. The Jap eased up close behind Uncle Leon and Uncle Leon turned quickly and slit the Jap's throat. After the ship came back to the States, Uncle Leon got off, came home, gave Grandpa his knife back and told him he got a Jap for him. Grandpa was so proud, but told him, "I wish you would have left the blood on it."

When I started writing this, I began thinking Grandpa was either 69 or 70 years old when he died in early 1945, but England couldn't have been in war when he was sixty years old, so I called J.P. and asked because he remembers so much better than I do. He said he remembers people talking about Grandpa lying about his age when he went to the recruiting office and told the officer he was sixty years old. He shaved his head to look younger; it didn't work.

Tallahala flooded one year and closed some of the roads around. As a kid, I never saw that happen before, but it made me think of Noah, one of the stories Mama use to read to us. It looked as though the seas and oceans were swallowing up all the earth. How high would the water come up before there is no more water? How will we be able survive when all we have will be under water? The men around that had boats got them out, got their guns out of the house, and headed for deep water looking for food that was running from the waters, heading for higher ground. I suppose it was harvest time for the lucky ones that had boats because I heard what they said and I saw when some of them came back in. All the rabbits, rats, and snakes and on and on that were on the little islands around in the woods and fields. I, being just a kid, thought when I got grown I too was going to have me a boat so I could be that lucky at hunting game. That big flood never came again as long as I lived near Tallahala.

There was a black lady living just down the road from us, and she had a son that was a little low in learning ability. He was large enough to be a grown man, yet his mother didn't seem to be far up in age to say she was old. J.P. and I would be around the Hodges grandparents' home and the lady would go by with her son, as she always had him with her. They could go by our house and be the same distance, but I don't think she would want to leave the road because part of the way she would have to go down a trail with no house close by for protection. Her son's name was Wyatt, very friendly to people they met. His mother would only smile as they passed, was in no hurry, while Wyatt would speak and seemed to wait for a friendly chat. Once they came by, J.P. said something about his wire that he was using to roll a lid of some kind down the road. Now, with a big smile he said, "I have another v-eight at home." That seemed to be his joy. Sometimes he had a long stick inside a syrup bucket and would push the bucket down the road. He was very amusing to us and we were probably equally amusing to him.

One evening J.P. and I heard some noise at a certain neighbor's house which was about a quarter of a mile from us. I couldn't understand any of the yelling going on, so had to ask J.P. if he knew what was said. He told me that our neighbor was having fun with Wyatt by using a whip to scare him into preaching and when Wyatt slowed down our neighbor would pop the whip, then Wyatt would start preaching again. J.P. or someone told me this certain neighbor would sometimes have him sing at the pop of the whip and, of course, the neighbor would have an audience and lot of laughing going on. I used to feel sorry for a mother that could not do a thing about it, but wait until the men had their fun and let them go home. Most of feeling sorry was for poor old Wyatt being taken advantage of just because he couldn't help being slow of mind, yet he had a happy personality at heart.

Word circulated that Wyatt and his mother, of which I cannot remember her name but I seem to think it was Mary and we will call her that, were walking down the road and passed our neighbor's house. The neighbor's dog ran out barking and running after them. When Mary ran to the field fence and started to climb through to get away from the dog, her underwear got hung on the barbed wire. With the dog closing in on her while one of the neighbors ran out and called the dog off until he could free Mary and be on their way. After all the laughs are over, and I have been able to think of how much of those tales I have heard really happened the way they were told. Well, I guess it has been so many years passed; what difference does it make? Besides that, a lot of people didn't wear under clothes very often in the hard times and she was a poor mother struggling to care for her son.

Sometimes I think of what we had to eat. At times we could go into the field and chew sugar cane when it got matured, eat peanuts at the right time, watermelons and different kinds of vegetables that we liked raw. There were other times we ate what we could get, not what we wanted. Buttermilk and cornbread was a full meal at times which was a good meal for me because I liked that. When the crops began growing, getting ripe, maybe waiting to be harvested, we had unwanted help. Sometimes the frost got into our sugar cane, crows got into our watermelons, skunks got into our peanuts, coons got into our corn, weather got into our tomatoes, rabbits got into our greens, bugs got into our peas, the squirrels got into our pecans, moles got into our potatoes, opossums got into our chickens, rats got all they could eat and the rest of us critters got the rest: the chickens, the farm animals and us. While the wild animals grew fat on our fields, we had meat to eat with our meals of poke salad, turnips or whatever we had. I think we ate well, not like we wanted, because today I can eat most anything without being too choosy of what I eat. I can enjoy eating almost anything when I sit down too, especially if it doesn't cost me anything.

I heard the story of Grandpa Carpenter being very much educated in comparison to some of the rest of us, and he was able to do so many things. One thing that stuck with me was that he made his own artificial lure for fishing and said he kept parts for his good hobby. I was questioning now, how did he use an artificial bait when I don't think reels were made that far back, and was told that he used a pole, tied a line on it and fished mostly around trees and bushes with a lure on the other end of the line. He would throw it where he thought a fish may be and shake it and begin pulling it in his own way of fishing. I wonder now if fishing from a boat or wade fishing wouldn't be the way to go. I sure don't have much luck with rod and reels.

Grandpa Carpenter did lots of things, and I don't know what all, but he was a preacher, teacher, farmer, tinker or peddler for I think Singer Sewing Machines and some kind of a circuit rider as he sold sewing machines. Selling sewing machines and preaching on his rounds made me wonder about him. Did he not make enough money for preaching in the churches on his route and had to work his way to pay for all the expenses? Or did he not make enough money on the sales he got from his sewing machines and had to pay for preaching in the churches? Or was he making good money by combining the two together?

I was told that one thing he got for his travels was my grandma. That is how they met. She had lost her first husband in some kind of accident before he found her, so she had a little boy. I guess he did well on the circuit, after twelve kids of his own with her, they stayed married.

J.P. was one of Grandpa Carpenter's pride and joy, and I guess that is why J.P. remembers him much better than I do. I feel I was just sort of there and didn't get the attention J.P. did, but I do remember when he had a pair of horses hitched to a hay mower. It seemed there were roots hung up on the blade and he stopped those horses, got down to do his work and him being in front of the mower, the horses started up, cutting his leg very bad. I would go see him while he was in the bed with that and would feel so bad for him.

Grandpa did his traveling in a horse drawn buggy. It was fun to ride on the back of that buggy. Now, I'm wondering how many of those boys had to walk to church, or did Grandma make Grandpa make trips home and back until he got all the family into the house of God?

Grandpa Johnny Hensarling, Maxine's Grandpa, told me about my Grandpa Carpenter going across Tallahala through a ford to get to the other side of the river. Now I am confused as to how to tell this next story because the

Runnelstown Baptist Church was where we grew up, so I guess he went to both churches at one time or another. Someone told me that there was to be a foot washing at the church and before Grandpa left the house, to get rid of the excitement some of the family slipped around and put soot inside Grandpa's socks. The source of this story, which I don't remember who it was, never heard of what the climax was after he got to church, but the story tells me Grandpa had a good sense of humor and fun to be close to. But someone else pictured him as a supervisor when it came to working. So he must have been more of a thinker and the family did most of the work, but for what I saw, he must have been a good planner. He did a good job raising my daddy, anyway.

We had a T-model Ford, the one that we had a wreck in once; my first car wreck. We were on our way to town and most roads were gravel then. I was one that liked to see where I am going, so the only way to do that was to sit on the edge of the seat, stretch out toward the windshield and look out. The steering wheel came loose from something and the car went out of control, down into the ditch. It went with me going through the windshield, as safety glass wasn't out yet in our cars. The most I remember was sitting on the curb where the doctor's office was, crying with all those bandages on my face and head, eating cornflakes with milk running down into the bandages and under my chin. Mama said the doctor ran his thumb nail into the wound by my eye and said the glass didn't quite go through, but I don't remember it.

I said all that to tell of the model-A, two-seater that the grandparents had at Grandpa's home at one time. Ford figured they saved a lot of money by not having a door on front for the driver, and one million dollars comes to mind, but I'm not too sure what it was. As kids would say now, "That looked real cool for the driver to jump from the ground up into the driver's seat." Now, I couldn't drive yet so I always had to sit on the back seat and not able to jump into the car. When it came time to go to the grist-mill, the Carpenters would tell Daddy or Mama that they would be going at a certain time on a given day and to be at their house if we wanted to go with them. We would shell corn, bag it up in a cloth bag that would hold about a peck and on to the grandparent's home we went and like they said if we missed the time, we also missed a ride. A peck of corn would get heavy after a three mile walk with it on my shoulder when I missed my ride to Runnelstown where the mill was.

After that, they had a truck and I don't remember what kind it was, but it had been around for a while. Wilber was the youngest of Daddy's brothers and he would drive it to Runnelstown. It was jimmy-rigged to where there was a wire between the toes with the short stick on top of Wilber's foot. That was a lot of fun, too.

Daddy said when we became a certain age, he was going to give us a calf to raise and make a little money as we grew up. For some reason, Alma Lee reached that age before the rest of us kids, so she got the first calf. She was really proud of what she got for growing up. As she grew up, she already had some fire in her blood. In fact, I thought at times Mama and Daddy figured she would be the first and last child and gave her all the hot temper the family could muster up and left the rest of us with mild tempers but, of course, my hot temper showed up later on. I sometimes wondered why she stood up for herself with Mama and Daddy when she knew they didn't like backtalk, but somehow she got by when I was afraid she would be talking herself into a lot of trouble. She felt good about the calf alright, until one sad day she had to give it up.

Daddy had tried planting a cover crop in the winter, and when spring came he would plow the winter peas under so to rot and be ready to plant our usual crops with a much healthy soil. Now someone told him about a better winter crop called vetch. Vetch is one of a kind of the winter pea variety. So, he got seed plus some kind of chemical to make the seed germinate, but it had something in it to be poison also. Daddy got his ground ready while we took care of persimmon sprouts and helped him carry seed and such to the field. "We" means Alma Lee and me. I don't remember why Alma Lee's calf was in the field, but she was there and went snooping around to see what we had there. When she saw the seed she reached it to help herself to what we had. Daddy saw her and went to waving his arms and talking to her with some French language loudly to get rid of her. He was mad and Alma Lee got a little mad at him talking like that to her friend. The heifer ran a few feet but she sure didn't want to leave that delicacy. She watched Daddy as she stood there hoping he would go on about his business and let her enjoy a little more of that good stuff. Daddy didn't have any kind of planter and his only way was to carry a bucket of seed and broadcast the seed was by hand. When he started to go, the heifer had business of her own. Daddy told us to drive that thing toward the lot to get rid of her and she wasn't far, when she started acting strange. The chemical had started to work. Soon she was very sick and lay down on the ground. Daddy stopped, looked back and went over to check her out, then realized she would never grow up to be a cow. Alma Lee started making her appearance and Daddy tried to make her understand the poison was in with the seed and he tried to keep the calf away from it, but as far as she was concerned there was no excuse for killing her heifer. She told him that he was going to have trouble with her until he paid her for the calf. I felt so bad that Alma Lee was getting too deep into trouble with Daddy. The calf died and Daddy told her he would pay her, I think to keep her quiet, but for us three to watch the thing die helplessly hurt all of us. Alma Lee took her time to let her temper cool. I don't remember Daddy buying seed for growing vetch again. Neither did he give Alma Lee another start for a herd of cows.

Alma Lee and I were like most other boys and their sisters, so there isn't much to say of interest, but I do remember a time when Alma Lee gave me a whipping. We had been aggravating each other, and it seems to be more aggravating to Mama more than it bothered us. Mama kept telling us to hold it down, and to us we had a good thing going. To us it was like eating peanuts. We just couldn't quit. We did go too far, and finally Mama just had enough. She said, "Alright, you two are waiting to fight, so we will just have it out right now." Now think. This was my Mama that taught us boys that we should keep our hands off of girls because they would break really easy. So we were growing up to be real gentlemen when we were around girls and it had its effects on us. I didn't want to fight with anyone, but much less my own sister. Besides that, she was helping to raise us boys. Mama got herself a switch off a hedge bush and after stripping the leaves off, stood there telling us to have at it. She said she wanted us to get it over with and behave ourselves. We waited for her to change her mind, but she said, "If you don't start fighting, I'm going to whip you until you do start fighting." Alma Lee came in on me with a whop to the stomach and I bent over with my hands on my wounded body. I heard Mama say, "Straighten up and hit her!" I just didn't want to make that machine mad anymore. Then I hear Mama calling for blood and Alma Lee came in on me again, and I still refused to make things worse than what I already had it. Mama never hit me with the switch but my stomach was sure sore from the punches that Alma Lee gave me for free. We had never come to blows before or after that experience. I wonder why Mama didn't teach Alma Lee never to lay hands on boys.

Daddy's brothers that were young and still at home with my grandparents, the Carpenters, rigged up a way to tell when the best fishing time was by a barometer. They didn't have one, so they made one of their own. They took a Coca-Cola bottle and found a jar with the right size mouth so the bottle would set upside down in without falling through, but just right to stick inside far enough to work for them. They put water in the jar, enough to go up part way into the neck of the Coca-Cola bottle, and a cork floating on top of the water where it would be easy to tell where the top of the water was. They put lines on the bottle at a place where the water rose and dropped, telling the barometric pressure and when the pressure got to the right line, they knew that the fish should bite and if time permitted they would go see if the thing was lying or not. Tallahala was close to them.

When Daddy went to the coast on a new job, he left us to farm without him, except on weekends, a lot of the time. Mama said that while Daddy was away making money for the family, we could hold down the farm. People usually planted corn in April and cotton in May. Mama said she believed that if we could plant corn in March we could get more time for it to grow before the hot weather came in on us, so that is what we did. Knowing that frost may bring in a killing sweep on our crop and people would start to laugh at us for being so stupid when after our bringing up we should be a lot smarter than that. Oh well, Mama said to let them laugh and they did before our crop had a chance to show anybody up. But as people say, a good laugh is good for our health. When we would be at church, would they laugh? What about when we would go to the store? Well, the corn sprouted and began to grow. The frost wasn't too rough on it and it began to show a good future. One good thing for us is that we had more time to pay attention to our cotton when it was time to plant it, and when cotton came up, the grass came with it and there was a lot more work to take care of it. As the corn's growth increased, the laughing decreased. When maturity came to the corn, the stalks were tall and the ears of corn were large. Now, where was all that laughter? Mama and we kids were happy. Daddy was happy. Now how did our neighbors feel? The spring of the next year, it seemed they were all trying to be the first to plant. They had called the Carpenters' corn winter corn, but not anymore. Now everybody wanted winter corn and no one was heard laughing.

After the corn was in the crib, Daddy gave some of the best corn to the pastor. That didn't go to well with Mama since Daddy didn't raise or harvest it. Was the corn a sacrifice? I don't know. Was it the tithe? I don't know. Was it the first born? I don't know if they tithed or not, because we were still affected by the depression, but at that time we were looking for a change in our finances. I don't remember much but I still know about the sweat to grow that corn.

One difference in the early corn is that the bud worms would hit the corn in the bud. We had to go down the rows after the corn got up, I don't know, maybe four or five feet high and hand pick the worms out of the tops of corn. The worms looked just like cut worms to me, and I still think they were the same. The corn that came on later at the usual time wouldn't be affected with those worms as bad.

The corn was up, and it came time to thin it out. We always put three kernels of seed to each hill on top of the fertilizer that was dropped in the furrow. Of course, I am going backwards with the planting but here is the way it went. Two of us worked together to plant the seed. One would step off with short steps, which were about three feet, and every time the second step was made, the one with the fertilizer would drop a tablespoon of the stuff and the one following would drop seed on top of the spot. When it came up and started to grow we would thin it out to leave one stalk to the hill. We always left the healthiest stalk to grow our corn.

Daddy told Alma Lee and me to bring our hoes to the field and thin the corn. Daddy always did the plowing and when the dirt started getting hot, Alma Lee and I started slowing down. All three of us were barefoot and the two of us wanted to go home. Daddy was barefoot too as I said, but he was walking behind the plow, in fresh plowed ground, which was pleasant to walk in. Alma Lee and I were cutting the corn low enough to pull fresh dirt out, enough to jump from one pile of fresh dirt to the next pile of fresh dirt, trying to keep our feet from baking in the hot dirt. Daddy saw us slowing down and told us how many rows we were going to have to thin before we could go in for lunch. That didn't make us kids very happy, so we kept going as we were. Finally, Daddy stepped out of the fresh dirt from the plow and into the hot, dry dirt and his feet started moving for a good shade. Daddy said to us that he didn't know that the ground was so hot and for us to go on to the house. Better words were never spoken. He didn't have to tell us twice. As soon as he told us he was sorry and that he didn't know it was so hot, we were on a dead run to the house. We were always barefoot and we were tough. But we had met our match, plus a little more. The hot dirt on our feet was more than we could cope with, but it was a pleasure to see that it got to our daddy, too. Now we know it was for real, and not just in our heads. It was on our feet. For the rest of the day for us just to lie around the house and do nothing was like a holiday.

Our home was built very well when it came to being tight in the winter time, but not that it was warm because our heating facilities were not like they are today, but all the ceiling was tight and air didn't go through beaded ceiling or beaded boards. Of course there seemed to have to be a breathing hole someplace. Mama and Daddy had fussed about the sound of rats in the overhead when all were suppose to be sleeping. After a few nights passed the noise started up and came above Mama and Daddy's bed. Now they are getting mad, and there was not a way to take care of the problem. Just when it looked that things couldn't get any worse, that rat relieved himself right where a crack was. That, of all places, was over Mama and Daddy's bed, and it went right in Daddy's face. He got up cursing and wiping his face, really getting himself a good workout. Mama was still in the bed, trying to not laugh but it came out anyway. As she tried to smother the laugh with all her might, Daddy thought she was crying and he started petting her and telling her everything was alright, and not to cry. By then, I think, everyone was awake, except me as I was too hard of hearing to let a little thing like that to wake me up when I was in a dream world. After all that loving and petting, telling Mama what he thought she wanted to hear, I don't think she ever told him the truth.

We had a dog that Daddy got from the Wedgeworth family that was a good hunting dog for anything with hair and meat on it. I wanted him to be a squirrel dog, not a dog for all things, but J.P. wanted a little meat for the table. One day we heard him in back of our field in a branch, and when we got there he had a rabbit in a hollow tree. J.P. and I argued about what we were going to do with the dog as to what we wanted the dog for. Rabbits or squirrels and we couldn't get together on the same idea. So I got a switch and reached inside the tree with it, twisted the rabbit's skin up with the switch and pulled it out of the hollow tree. The way I was going to break the dog from running rabbits was to turn the rabbit loose and whip the dog as he watched the rabbit run off, to let him know not to run those rabbits but chase the squirrels. I did that while J.P. watched. As the rabbit ran for his life, I used the same switch to whip the dog and tell him, "Do not run after the rabbit." I guess the dog thought I was telling him that I wanted him to love that critter. Well, he already did love that rabbit and all the other critters as soon as they were dead. We always gave the dog parts of the rabbits when we skinned them, like the guts, head, skin, feet and all of what we didn't eat after the poor devil did all the work to catch the rascal knowing we kept the good parts to eat ourselves. When I made known what I wanted and we were still fussing, I walked on out into the field and toward the house when I heard that dog barking again. I gave up. I knew I had lost the battle. Either way we were still able to eat meat, and I went on home. After some time later, J.P.'s dog and the same rabbit came on home and no doubt J.P. used the same switch I used to pull the same varmint out of the hollow tree before to pull him out of another tree and now they all came home together.

I wanted so much to become a man and go hunting alone and fishing just like grownups did. Finally the parents said yes, I could go head lighting for the rabbits but don't kill a cow. Now, I had to act like a man and don't shoot the wrong thing. I thought that day would never come but here we are, the right day and right night for me. I got the carbide light, the carbide and water in the light and my gun. Now, where is that rabbit? I knew that bay, just north of us, was open good where large trees were and good hunting for squirrels because of being open like it was a man could see a good long ways. Now, my main worry was to not get turned around and lose my way; to see where the moon was, the direction I would be walking, so I could make it back home. I didn't want to have to sit around, waiting for the daylight to come and go home a little late. It has always been easy for me to get turned around and get lost. In fact, I learned just where the North Star is by the position of the Big Dipper. Sometimes it doesn't show up, even though it could be on a bright sky night. The Big Dipper rotates as we see it, around the North Star. That is only one thing that I had to learn about night hunting. Then I had to stay on the road and cow trails until I got my education for night hunting. Now, let's see. I had to go down this lane until it makes a turn and now pick up the right cow trail until I got to the middle of the bay; turn left where the lay of the land shows where the water ran after the rain. Now, don't get off this map I have created in my mind. I hunted slowly on my way. Boy! I didn't realize a spider's eye would shine so bright, and there are so many of them! How would I know a rabbit's eye when I saw it?! I know that I would have to examine those eyes very closely. When I saw a very interesting eye shine in front of my light, I eased the safety off of my gun, slowly using my gun sight, slowly easing the trigger back and firing my first time in night hunting. I didn't wait for the smoke to clear. I just went out to pick up my kill, but there was not anything to be found. Well, now I had to go home and face Daddy, but I didn't want to. I didn't have to say the first words because he was waiting to ask me the first words and did. "What did you kill?"

"I don't know what I shot at because I couldn't find anything."

Daddy said, "Well if you don't get something the next shot, you can't go anymore. That was just a spider's eye you shot."

I felt bad. Now, how does he know that I shot a spider's eye when he wasn't even there? How would I know which is a spider's eye when there are some small and some large like the one I shot?

There was another good night just waiting on me. I was afraid to try, and yet I wanted to go try once more. I did the same thing as I done before, even though I had this mixed feeling about doing something wrong again.

When I got to the bay, I took a left and followed the hollow where the water ran, being very quiet not to make a mistake and cause any noise. Whoa! There was something different just waiting to see what I was going to do. I just wish I could say it like I saw it, to be able to show what I was looking at. The thing looked about the size of a cigar. It was as round and red as a cigar or would be if it was lit and had enough moving air on it to keep it burning. I looked at that reflection, hoping to see what was wearing that reflection, but nothing showed up. No cow, no hog or anything. My heart was giving me a whipping. So, I had to do something or go back home after giving up. What to do, what to do? Well, I was taking a chance but here goes. I raised the gun slowly, took a good aim, hoped real hard and fired. There I was, waiting for something to run or the smoke to clear, then slowly walked in the direction after the smoke cleared. I walked upon the largest cane-cutter, swamp rabbit I had ever seen. With that load, the way home was a far piece away but I had the joy of showing off my prize catch and I never had to ask if I could go night hunting for rabbits anymore. The shells for the gun was high priced but we brought in the meat for the table.

There are many things that we will always remember about some things, above other things we did in the past, and I wonder why we put some of those things in our memory bank, period. So very simple, so cultural, so unnecessary and this is one of the things I think of most, I guess. I don't remember my Daddy taking me hunting more than once but the once I do remember is when he killed six squirrels and one rabbit. I don't know if I was good or if I was bad. I could have been too young and I know I was hard of hearing. Either of those things could have been a handicap on my part, but my daddy never let me know if I made a mistake and I came home full of joy because I was taken hunting by my daddy.

The most I remember was when he said quietly, "Shhhhhhhhh!" After stopping I couldn't hear anything, and we both stood still watching for something, I didn't know for what. We were on the bank of a branch, and soon a rabbit came hopping by on the other side of the branch. Daddy moved very slowly with his gun, going up to his shoulder, taking a slow aim and squeezing the trigger. We went home with a few meals to eat. My desire was to be like Daddy.

One thing I learned about night hunting alone the hard way was the owls. The first time, this is what happened. I saw that my carbide light was on its way out. So I picked out a good spot that was clear enough, that I wouldn't be sitting on a rattlesnake when I cut the light off. The good thing about using carbide light was that it always gave a man plenty of time to look for a good place to be in the dark when it was time to reload. I got to a good place where it was clear and to keep from forgetting my bearings, I faced the route I was taking so when I got up I would know where south, the way home, and north, east and the west would always be the same. Then I knew where my direction would be. I pulled out my carbide, my water bottle, got a stick to dig out all the mud that the spent charged would have made and either sat or squatted down and blew out the light and recharged. Once the bowl was cleaned out, the carbide would go in and the water would be added so to have the water tank kept full, and not to have to worry about running out of light for awhile. Up in a tree, above my head, was a sound, "Owo-o-o-o-o-a-a—who, who, who,

who,-ah-h-h-h-h." My whole body wanted to move, and I had a lot of trouble keeping my moving parts from moving. Being raised up around there, I knew what it was but doubt kept trying to move in on me. I finally won out and charged my light up as fast as I could, and after getting it lit I tried to find that owl, but never could. It may have gone to some other tree. I couldn't forget that bird. He was very lucky that I couldn't find him resting on a limb, close to my shot gun. I had those chilling feelings all the way home. Would you believe the next owl that pulled that trick on me made me feel the same way? It sounded as though it was a woman screaming and my feet really wanted to move. I had to clean up my light and put in a new charge, there in those dark woods before I could go anyplace. I don't remember if I had any rabbits or not either time, but I remember the owl. Maybe, the owl was more important. It seems as if the clear area was the owl's watching spot where he could have plenty of room to sweep down on its prey when it started crossing the spot or was feeding around there. Owls, after that, never got to me that bad, but the dark makes a difference for if it had been daylight there would have been no fear.

Ralph and I had some throw lines we had thrown out in the river, and we thought it time to check and see if the fish were biting. We always liked to take worms, crawfish or both to bait up with. The spot where we had our lines is the spot that it seemed no one else wanted for some reason, and I think we were about to find out why. About a mile plus some, with bait and whatever else we thought we needed would start getting pretty heavy before the end of the line, that's for sure. When we did get there and checked our line it was hung up on a log or something. Being kids, we did not want to go out into that water to see what things looked liked down under and didn't want to find out how deep it was either, without knowing how to swim. We walked upstream and back down the river and still nothing changed. We found that Nolly and Roland had a boat tied to a tree close by and we wanted it pretty bad. Ralph couldn't see why we couldn't borrow it to check our line, but I held out for a while saying that we were to ask first if we could use it. Ralph was a little older and a lot more persuading than I was, so we checked it out and found out it also had a padlock on it. Now we argued some more because we had an axe with us, for some reason, maybe it was to cut the line. We finally cut the limb the chain was locked to and were on our way to the line. My memory is trying to say the weight we used was in the fork of a tree down under that kept our line from turning loose and we did get our line back, and also the boat, but yes, that boat. We still had a locked lock on that chain and were having a hard time trying to figure how to put the chain back on the tree. The trouble was getting close enough to the bank with that boat now, because the chain wasn't long enough now. Finally, we had everything figured out and had it tight enough to hold it. As we started walking back to our line, there were the two men coming to check their lines and they had caught us with their boat. Ralph was trying to make them understand why we were with their boat but they just stood there looking at us. I don't remember either of them saying a word, just standing there and looking. We went on to our line we had un-hung to take care of it, and never saw them again on that trip. It was never brought up anymore. "Be sure your sins will find you out"? Later, a few years after that,

I heard that boatmen had a code that when a man was caught stealing a boat the word would get around and he would never be able to own a boat. If he tried, it would be destroyed.

Calvin Broadhead and I cut some wood for a man that lived on Mr. Brown's place where our mailboxes were lined up on Highway 29. We cut and hauled it to his house, stacked it then waited for our money. Calvin was at his house to receive our pay. When the man came out of his house, he looked it over and told Calvin the stack had too many holes in it and he thought we should cut, haul and stack a good stack of wood so he would have a good cord. Calvin told me that he said to the man the holes were already there, so we just stacked the wood around the holes. I asked Calvin if we should cut more wood to please him and he said no, that he had a good cord but he was just trying to get more wood for his money. The guy did go ahead and pay us our money though. I don't remember much of what was said between them, I wasn't with the two but as long as I got my money everything was ok with me. I wish I could remember the customer's name but it seems that I waited too long to write this down to expect my brain to kick in and throw that back at me.

Electric fences may have existed for a long time before we heard about them. After we started hearing that they were for real for the people who had a need for controlling animals very easily where they were, where they should be, whether they should be inside or out, the control fences became a very interesting conversation piece. Having no electricity, the first fences were run by a battery, but later we did have electricity come through our part of the country. Mr. Miller lived on top of the hill leading out of Runnelstown east on Highway 42. Beside his house, he had a watermelon patch. To keep out somebody's animals from the watermelons, he fixed himself an electric wire to run around those goodies he was raising, and he, being one of the fellows that had electricity early after the company supplied power through there, ran power from his house, not from a battery. Now, this isn't the way to put power into a fence where cows, mules or any animals are controlled. 110 volts are just too much. When the electrical power came to us from a company that made the stuff for the first time, how were we to know how much is too much? He had a problem and he came face to face with the no-stock law on cows and he had some ideas of his own. Well, he got his fence charged up from his house. He looked up out across the yard and into his watermelons and saw his mule astraddle his new fence wire, just rocking back and forth, one side and then the other side. Before he could cut off the power and get his mule free the poor thing died a free mule. It was free from work, pain from anybodies' controlled fences, now resting from all of life's disappointments.

Webber Broadhead, a teen neighbor, went fishing in Leaf River as an all night trip with Lee Travis, Dunk Carter and I don't remember who else was in the group. While down there catching fish they found an alligator. There were no gun laws back then that would match the laws we have today, and sometimes we would take a gun because of snakes. They had a gun with them at the time and used it and brought back some alligator meat. They divided it up as per family that were represented and not by the number of people on the fishing trip, like they would do on a deer hunt. I was at the Broadhead's home much of the time and the boys in the home were at our house much of the time, and when the alligator meat came in the family cooked it up. Me, being there, they gave me some to let me find out what it tasted like. Was J.P. there? I don't remember, but I was ready for some of that delicacy. Almost 60 years later, I tasted of that good ole delicacy again and found out I still like it.

It seems strange how our culture was so different here in the United States when we were kids. We didn't know much about holidays except for Christmas and the Fourth of July. We farmed the land on the hill, that I mentioned before, and it was a sharecrop situation. Labor Day came at the time that our crop of string beans came into maturity and was ready to be picked or lost, whichever our priority called for. When we went to pick the beans, Alma Lee was kind of mad at Daddy because other people were taking a day off for Labor Day, but not us. We had to keep working. We were at an age that we could not understand what we should know. The owner of the land also had a family, but none of that family ever worked that land. She felt bad that even though the land belonged to someone else we had to do all the work. I don't think I had ever heard of Labor Day. I don't recall it anyway. I asked Alma Lee, "What is Labor Day?" She told me what it was, and then I felt bad. We missed a lot I guess, like April's Fool, Trick or Treat, shivaree and such, when the rest of the world was running off and leaving us. Even after I was grown, Maxine and I moved to Texas. Someone asked me if I was going to celebrate Juneteenth, and I asked, "What is that?"

He said, "You know what that is."

I said, "I have never heard of it."

He then asked, "Do people in Mississippi ever take off for that day?"

I said, "No, I sure don't think so. I guess we must not have had it."

So, the boys told me what it was. I told them, I had not heard of that before, and we sure didn't do it in Mississippi. If the employers gave that to white people, I sure could use a lot of Juneteenths.

Uncle Leon had brought two monkeys home on a ship and one was for Mark. Grandpa Hodges had built their home, a two story building and didn't put in any inside wall in the upstairs part of it. My grandma was cold natured, grandpa was hot natured so he slept upstairs so that he could feel the cool air that came through the windows. Grandma slept downstairs so that she could be warm. The monkey slept under the overhang that Grandpa built on the side of the house as a shade to keep some outside stuff sheltered from the weather. He had a box fixed like a hen nest so there could be comfort for the little critter. He also had a long enough chain so that he could be free to go a little distance but confined enough to keep him from getting ideas and keep him from being killed by some animal running wild. Of course, Mark slept downstairs. A blue northern blew in and things began to get cold. Everybody was comfortable where they slept. No worries. That is until the chill became cold and Grandpa figured out he was tough, but nature had shown up mad, bringing wind and ice along with it. He found his way down to Grandma's bed. Now, Grandma was a small woman and there wasn't heat there but that feather bed felt good so he wasn't in any hurry to leave it. Grandma and Mark made out ok but the monkey, well nature was too rough on the poor thing. It got inside the nest box and left his tail hanging out, and during the night that tail died. Frozen. It wouldn't even move any more. Grandpa waited for a time and the tail just didn't look good. He knew the thing had not made it alive, so he got his pocket knife and a hammer. He went out to the monkey, gave him a bite to eat to keep his mind off what Grandpa was doing, and got the monkey's tail on the wood part of the box, under the doorway and into the box. He put his knife blade on the dead tail to where it joined the live part and hit the knife with the hammer. Now the monkey had lost that part of his tail. Grandpa said he didn't even flinch. He was rid of some dead weight. From then on, he was a bobbed tail monkey that never changed his lifestyle from the ordeal.

Daddy had bees at one time, but I don't think it lasted very long. I don't remember him and Mama harvesting the honey but one time.

Daddy sawed down a hollow gum tree and sawed a block from it at the size he wanted for the bees he had, enough room to take care of man and bees. In and above the bottom became the brood chamber he had holes bored to where he could cross some round sticks for support for the wax. On the bottom was a notch where it was to sit on a board for the bees to be able to go in and out of the hive. He also put a board on the top to cover it with. He put bees in and waited for the bees to have a brood coming along to build up the bees' population. Now the bees had to have a little time to do their thing. When it seemed to be enough honey in the hive Daddy and Mama went out with a screen wire wrapped across their faces, pulled the top board off and using a sharp knife started cutting cones of honey out of the hive. We kids had the windows closed in the house with our noses up to the glass where we could watch all the fun and still be away from the bees. The cone that was cut out was put in a pot with a lid and when they were finished, the honey was taken in to the kitchen to process. The honey was extracted by using cheese cloth, squeezing it out by hand. I know, now, how the honey would run down into the brood section and bees would get messed up in honey, the other bees wouldn't help them get cleaned up. I am sure the bees either moved or died. Using the gum tree for the hive is where the name "Bee-Gum" came from, instead of using the word hive.

Aunt Sue Chapel was Daddy's mother's sister. She smoked a corncob pipe. She was known to us as "Aunt Sue that smoked a pipe" and any of the family knew who we were referring to. To me, she was a nice old lady and just another part of the family. She had that strong, smooth way of saying things that kind of made me listen to her because it sounded as it was something worth listening to like our Grandma Carpenter. She didn't talk much to us kids, but it seemed like she felt like we belonged there; not like we were much of a bother, but part of life. Just nice.

Daddy decided to take J.P and me to the old eddy. I think he liked to go back there because he had lived around there all his life and had memories about the lake. He just liked to see if it was still there. We boys were so proud that our daddy was going with us and swim just like we did. The long walk was great, just feeling like we were somebody because it seemed to be that we only got to go to church with him, but "look at us now". Down the road, through the woods and seeing the water's edge at the end of the trail made us feel like running to the jumping in point, take off our clothes and jump in. As we got to the old eddy and started making our way around the north side and looking at the sandbar on the south, a long way from any road but deep in to the woods, who did we see? Aunt Sue, the aunt that was a bit older than Daddy, fishing away and smoking her corn cob pipe. We all three stopped and the two grownups chatted for awhile. Then she said for us boys to go on and swim, but Dad did not want to scare the fish when two naked boys hit the water with a loud splash.

She said that the fish weren't biting anyway so Daddy said, "Go on in. She has seen naked boys before."

Now, my mama taught us better than that. Aunt Sue said, "Yeah, I've seen a lot of naked boys before so just don't pay me no mind and I want pay you any."

That wasn't good enough for me, but I didn't know what J.P. was thinking. We just stood there looking at each other.

Daddy said, "Go on in. She doesn't care."

We slowly turned to look at the trail and then back at them and I wondered, now if she has seen that many boys, why doesn't Daddy go on in with us? He reminded us to go on to the sand bar and jump in, so we slowly went on our way and were straight across the lake from the grown-ups. J.P. and I kept looking at each other with a glance as if to say, "Help!"

When we got to the other side we went into the bushes and downed our breeches, wondering what our mama was going to think about us and hoping we would not get a whipping for such a nasty thing. At the same time we knew our daddy would protect us if he was there when she found out, but what if he wasn't there? She wouldn't believe that! We sneaked out from behind those bushes in hopes the smoke from her old corncob pipe was in her eyes while we held our hands in front of our privates until we got them under the water. We couldn't enjoy any fun until Aunt Sue got tired of fishing and talking with Daddy, and got up and say good-bye to each other.

Daddy came around the lake where we were and sat down on the ground where it tapered off toward the water's edge and asked, "Are you boys about ready to get your clothes on and go home?" We hadn't even swam on top of the water yet because our hind ends may stick up high enough for Aunt Sue to see us. We just didn't think about that being too far to show anything to her, and we were playing it safe. We had chores to do so another trip was ruined, and we had a feeling of hopelessness and disappointment because we were in the presence of a lady. Now, the lady who was at home waiting for our return never said anything to us about our day at the lake, so maybe she still didn't know that we were showing off while Daddy and Aunt Sue talked.

Mama, Grandma Hodges, J.P. and I think Alma Lee and I went into the bay in the southeast of our home to pick May halls for jelly when they were ripe. We didn't have long to get what we could before they rotted because May halls were usually around where water set for long periods of time and they just didn't last but a short time.

The May hall trees had thorns and when a limb fell into the water it sometimes found a way to work a thorn in the bottom of a bare foot, and we did go into the water without shoes on. After all, it was in the summer time and as growing children we usually out grew those "once a year shoes" by May hall picking time. We could not see much of the bottom because of so many leaves that fell in and had not rotted yet. We also knew that snakes were in and out of those wet places, but we didn't worry much about them until we saw one. We were careful though, where we walked because of thorns and snakes, particularly at this type of place. For thorns we would kind of slide our feet along the bottom under the leaves. Of course, when we mudded up the water we couldn't help that.

This part of the bay ran from our land into what we called the Mack Carter land. We had found and gotten rid of a Lamprey eel and I was very careful not to let it live or get too close to my feet. I didn't know it didn't have jaws but a sucking mouth. It was a large eel, more so maybe in that water. I was hoping to hurry and finish picking May halls before the worst came upon us, when we heard someone yelling something I could not understand. We all stopped and looked up to see what the excitement was all about and saw Mack's mother yelling at us. I asked what was she saying and someone said she was telling us to get off her property. The rest of our family kept picking up May halls and I asked if we should go, but Grandma said no. She started yelling the best she could which wasn't good enough to hear her more than thirty feet and said we were not black people, all is alright, etc. I was looking for my ears to pick up some sounds of gunshots, and I think I was the only one not doing my work. Grandma was telling us Mrs. Carter thought we were black, so all was okay. The Carter family was our next door neighbors. What now? No one had up "No Trespassing" signs anyway. Nothing ever happened except we got more May halls.

There was a black man that raped a white woman. The law found out who he was, found him, took him to the jail, locked him up and left him there alone. There were some men who got together to break him out and did just that. They took him down to Pearl River, I don't know whether he was dead or alive when the men got there, but his body was thrown into the water. The sheriff and his people looked for the black guy for some time, and in some way they learned where he was thrown in. They tried looking in the river for him but were not having any luck. Someone told the sheriff and his men to take a bundle of corn fodder and throw it in the place the body was thrown in. They got a bundle of fodder, threw it in the place where the body was thrown into the water, and followed the fodder where ever it went and it led them to where the body had hung up on some logs or something down in the water. Some said that when they drug him out he had bleached white. The story goes that the practice of throwing the fodder in the water to find a dead body was an old ritual that had been used in time past. I wonder did the Indians think of that and pass it on to the white man some long time before? Some of our ideas did come from them.

When we planted soy-beans and raised them for cow feed, we harvested differently than anything else. We cut the stalks, put them on the ground in rows where they would accept the heat from the sun and would be an easy chore to pick them up and take them to the barn. They didn't need to be cut over a day or two in the heat of the summer in order to dry enough for them to keep from molding. We timed the harvest according to the full moon so we could wait until the dew covered the leaves enough to be wet and take one arm load at a time to the shelter. The soy-beans were raised close to the barn and we didn't have the space we needed, so it never was a long time job. We didn't like to work with Daddy at night, and we would get very sleepy before we quit so went in the house. We should have carried the stalks in during the daylight. The leaves would have shed off and our roughage would have been lost. The cows would still chew on the tender part of the stalks when the leaves were gone, but the good stuff was assumed to be in the leaves where the best food was. I never liked to work, but after the sun went down no one should have to work.

Pea vines made good hay even without leaves. We did not have the transportation to do what we needed to do. If we had, then we could have carried soy-beans and pea vines to a feed mill and had it milled and mixed with other feed and made it into sack feed. We had to do with what we had.

Some of the times we would catch the cornstalk and pull the fodder, tie it in bundles where they would shed water when it rained and would not sour. We would pull the fodder when the ears of corn were ripe and starting to dry. If the corn was too green the ears of corn would hurt, we couldn't wait too long or else the food value in the fodder would hurt. Peanuts were pulled and stashed around a pole, then a piece of plywood or sheet of masonite or maybe even a sheet of roofing tin, was placed on top to help keep the water from going down inside the shock. Hay and straw also was put in a shock around a pole.

I keep thinking as I tell these stories of the old ground slides we used to have. Daddy made the first one that I remember and I built the last one that I can remember at the time, but it lasted most of my childhood days. We couldn't afford a wagon and Uncle Oren gave Daddy some old log wagon wheels which Daddy used to make a two wheel cart that we were so happy with. The slide served its purpose through the years. I think about my imagination back in my childhood days and about those simple little things like being in a race with other mules and slides, putting seats on them, putting lights on the slides and, of course, the mule, and riding through the country caroling at Christmas time, riding the slide like the people in old times in the chariots inside the arenas before crowds of people.

I don't know why we called those things slides. Was it just because we were taught that or were they really called that? What about a sled? Is that the same thing? At Christmas time people sing about a one horse open sleigh. Is there a difference? What is meant by open? Is it a vehicle on runners and closed up like an automobile, but they run at Christmas with the windows open? I think I will still call it a ground slide.

I never saw a mule get spooked when she was pulling one, but I did wonder what would have happened to her and the slide. I just thought of her hurting herself. Within my mind, I could see the slide being tossed about, sometimes waving in the air. Of course, that would be after I had gotten off. When we hitched the mule to the ground slide, we were not rolling along, just sliding around.

The way it was made was with two 2x6 boards, about six or maybe eight feet long for the runners, tapered on the front so the slide will not hit a root or anything rising above the ground, but would slide over the ground with ease. The runners were set up to be six inches high and boards nailed on it and a little bracing was in place so it would be strong and sturdy.

We used it for most of what a wagon would be used for. When it wasn't loaded we rode standing up. The runners had a chain on front from one runner to the next and had a single tree for hooking the mule to it so she could pull it. The slide was very good for bringing wood home, and fertilizer came in one hundred pound sacks, so it worked well for hauling that. We used it for feed, and maybe just for a ride. A wagon lobs along over ruts, rows, things that make the ground rough or anything that makes the wagon jerk up and down making the ride very unpleasant, but a slide? Smooth as silk. A wheel goes into the holes, a runner on a slide reaches across most of the holes.

When we needed to haul something like watermelons or maybe tubs of vegetables, anything of the sort, we would nail up side bards with whatever we could find. Sometimes it would be broken cypress pickets from the yard fence and nails from under the wash pot to box it in. Instead of a one horse open sleigh, it would be a "one mule open basket."

We boys hauled out many cords of wood for us and other people. Just sliding along making new trails from the woods to home with wood that was going to cook our food and warm our other side. It's strange that as a kid I could saw wood and split it all day but to use that cross cut saw now, I would have to rest several times to make one tree fall to the ground.

Carter's Grocery Store still standing!

We Believed . . .

People believed when a person was deathly ill, if an owl would go to the house and call out at night, and it was a Screech Owl, there was a death about to happen to someone.

When an old person died, there was soon to be rain.

We heard stories about when a dead person was left at a wake alone at night rats would feed on the body. Once, I heard that a cat was caught eating flesh from a lady. Was it true? I don't know.

When looking up at the moon at night, if there was a quarter moon crescent shaped, the cup shape points were as if it would hold water, rain wasn't to be. If it pointed down as if it would not hold water, the rain was to be because the moon was pouring out water.

Plant the crops according to the moon: some in the growing of the moon, some in the full moon and some in the decrease of the moon. If it was fruit below the ground, it would be in the dark of the moon.

When killing a snake, lay it on its back, leave it that way and other snakes wouldn't stay around.

We were to plant some cut potatoes when we kids were small. Dad had cut the potatoes with so many eyes on each section, and pushed the cut part down into ashes for some reason; that made them get a better start. When we were ready to drop these in the furrows, I remember someone in the family mentioning to Dad the reason we were careful how the potato hit the grown. It was because some people said if the eye was looking down when the sprout came out of the potato to start growing it would go down, but if it was looking up, it would come out of the ground like it should. Dad said, "The sprouts know which way to come up, now don't waste any more time and plant them in the fresh dirt before the dirt gets dry." I think Mama was the one that told Dad how she thought they should be planted, but to Dad that was right.

Daddy once got some cedar bushes to set out in front of the house. We kids told Daddy we didn't want him to transplant the cedar and, of course, he wanted to know why. We told him we had heard that when someone transplanted a cedar tree, the planter would die when it grew enough to shade his grave. He planted; he lived.

Marvin Carpenter and his first wife,
Maxine Hutson Carpenter

Back Then

My mama raised us boys up to miss a lot of fun—with the girls, that is. She thought that we should look at them but to never fight, hit, hug or hold hands with them, and they should be looked up to. When I got old enough to pay attention to them, I was kind of confused. There have always been people who would sneak under the cover of love, but not with MY mama around! We, being her kids, were the only ones she raised and I guess she was going to do a good job with what she had. I really don't know what she taught the girls. I could never understand how we were born to the same mom and dad, yet boys were to look up to girls because they were weak, special and needed protection, but never touched.

I remember the first time I visited a young lady's home. I was nervous from the time I left the house. Of course we walked every place, so a girlfriend would have to live close by or else she would not be visited. She lived in a house on Mac Carter's place. Her name was Marie Ikard. Her daddy worked with a circus and was away from home a lot. When I knocked on the door, one of the girls came to the door. Because of my age, everyone knew who I wanted to see. Marie came out, shut the door behind her and offered me a seat on the porch swing. I sat down on one end then she sat on the other end. Now what? I didn't know what I was supposed to say, and I guess she didn't know what I was suppose to say either because she didn't help me with my part of the play and things got a little quiet around there. The darkness was on our side, but how did we know? We were in untraveled territory with no guide to help us to explore the restless expedition we got ourselves into. Her mama was just on the other side of the wall where the window was and she could not see or hear anything going on either. She just had to know what was going on and where we were so she called Marie and asked her if all was OK.

Marie said, "Yes, Mama." Now, I don't know who was the most nervous; Mama, Marie or me. Now I had two problems. What was I to do or say to my lady friend, and now Mama had become my other problem. Should we talk about the weather or what? We didn't know much about weather, and if we did, there was nothing we could do about it. Besides that we took what came without any surprises because we knew that the weather changes, changes were going to come, and we lived on accordingly, regardless of what kind of weather we got. We didn't like school so that wasn't a good subject to talk about. Who wants to talk about picking cotton or whatever?

Here comes Mama's voice again, "Marie, what are you all doing?"

Marie assured Mama, "We ain't doing anything, Mama."

Marie was right, but we both wished we weren't so bashful. We didn't know how to misbehave so we stayed on our end of the porch swing wishing we knew what to do. We didn't want embarrassment to come between us, but we were confused not knowing what to do next. My mama would have been proud of me, just sitting there with my hands in my pockets or wherever they were. Sometimes my hands were in the way. I didn't know what to do with them. It was like when I smoked for a few years and then quit. I found that there was no place to put my hands and make them fit. Marie wouldn't lead in conversations so I couldn't tell just what she was thinking. Her mother must not have known what she was thinking either, but maybe thought that she had guessed what Marie had on her mind because she kept calling Marie through the window wanting to know what she was doing. Marie kept saying, "We ain't doing nothing, Mama!" I had the feeling that I might have been in the wrong place, maybe in the way, and Mama may have been more able to see through the window and into the dark. I told her goodnight and Marie sounded as if she might have been getting mad at Mama or me so I headed for home where I could find a little more comfort waiting for me. I wondered if all mamas were afraid to let a nice, young man like me visit their girls after dark without making them feel that the police department was keeping an eye on the situation.

Time passed. We saw each other at school or at someone's party, but that mama never had to worry about me after that.

At school and church we were always around the girls, but I never put my hands on one except holding hands in a game at a party. But even if my hands were not on them, my eyes were. I didn't know how to be bad either. My mama wouldn't let me learn how. I looked at the girls as if they were a kitty cat, but wouldn't get close to them, afraid to take chances that they may turn into an alligator and try to devour me I guess.

When we took a girl to a party at some home in the neighborhood, we had to walk. It was very boring so I didn't date much. I would walk in one rut in the road, and my date would walk in the other. When I got ideas, I would see my mama's spirit in my mind, as if she were watching me. I don't know if she was even thinking about me, and yet she may have been praying for me. I don't know. We didn't have any stock laws on cows and when the darkness came before we took our walk, we were in constant fear of stepping in something the cows had left behind.

When I got prepared to go courting, I would try to go by the store first and buy a pack of gum, which had five pieces in it, for a nickel. I would break one piece of gum and stick it back in the pack to make it look like a full pack unhampered with. That way I had enough for two dates; one whole piece for her each time, and one half-piece for me. Then I would still have a whole piece of gum left.

Once I was at school in the auditorium where we sometimes had a study period between classes. In the auditorium there was a stage, with a small room on each side with an entrance to the stage, also used for storage. I went into one of the rooms for something. I turned and saw one of the girls in my class follow me in, turn around, and close the door. I stepped back and waited for her to walk past me to get whatever it was she needed. She walked up to me, put her arms around me and we came mouth to mouth. I looked toward the shut door wondering when someone would be coming inside and tried to turn away from her, but she stuck on. I relaxed and held back, realizing it felt pretty good. Before she turned me loose and let me go, I just learned where sugar came from and why God loved all the girls. I came to be on God's side as I changed my mind. I've never been the same. I had a new friend.

I forgot what it was she was in that room for and I still don't remember if I ever knew. She may have forgotten also, but I'm not sure. Maybe she got what she wanted, just a little attention between classes.

City Life

I remember going to town before we had parking meters to time how long a car would be parked in a designated area where people needed to do business, finish and move on so someone else could park in the same spot. They, too, needed to do business and move on for somebody else. The city had other ways to keep people moving on. The police department would assign a man in different areas to walk down so many streets to keep traffic moving. He had a special stick that held a piece of chalk fitted on the end so he wouldn't have to bend over to mark the tires of the park cars which saved a lot of time. The tire would be marked on the tread to where when the car moved out, the mark would wear off before he was ready to stop and park again. When the police made his round an hour later, and a car with a mark on his tire, he got a winning ticket . . . for the city that is. People learned that if they needed to be in the same place longer than an hour, all he needed to do was pull up a little where the mark would be on the ground, the policeman wouldn't see it, and the owner of the car would save getting a ticket for over parking. After that, the policeman would try to see the change in the car's position.

Milk, back then, was delivered by a delivery truck from house to house. Someone who wanted milk would put the empty milk jugs out on the porch steps out front with a note in one of them, telling the delivery man how many of what was needed for that day. If he did not see a milk bottle out on the front, he wouldn't stop, which saved him time. Of course, this was for only the city people.

No one had refrigerators back then. A few did have an ice box that the ice was put in the top part of the box and food was kept under the ice compartment, so they could buy ice and keep them cool longer. Otherwise, the milk would only be good for that one day.

Now the country people were different. Some of the people living in the country who didn't have a cow could sometimes borrow a milk cow from a good hearted neighbor for their milk until the cow went dry. Some were able to swap that cow back to the owner and borrow another cow that would still give milk. The borrower would feed the cow and the calf for the time he had one on loan. The calf would grow during the time of its stay so the owner wasn't losing anything.

When country people dug wells they could put milk in a jar, tie a rope on it and lower the milk into the cool water below and the milk would last longer. That's country living. Now, back to city living.

There were ice trucks, as they were called back then, and their routes were far from the ice houses and they went from house to house to deliver the ice. Their truck beds had a pile of saw dust they used to keep the ice from melting down. They'd go to the ice supply company, buy the ice, and put it in the ice box if one was there. If not, they would put it in a tub with saw dust in it to keep ice in or a quilt to cover it inside the tub.

Sometimes, someone would run a route in the country, but never stayed very long because there was not enough money to feed a family very long. Too much time was spent from house to house and making too many stops without a sale.

In Hattiesburg, there was a man named Bowear, or was so called, and he was somewhat on the heavy side. So, when he walked down the street he kind of swayed back and forth as he was selling peanuts in small bags. They were parched and some people bought some because they knew he made a living from the sale of peanuts. I never knew much about him, even though he was laughed about, a known figure on the streets of Hattiesburg, and was said to be some kind of a lookout for the police.

There was also a lady who walked the streets of Hattiesburg with a winter coat on, even in the summer time, selling boiled peanuts. She was called Miss Hattiesburg. She too was often seen and was laughed about. A person could mention either of the two of the people and anyone would know who was being talked about. I felt sorry that these two people probably had to do something like that to make a living, while others would use them for a joke. I never knew what happened to either of them.

A lady reminded me of the old street cars in New Orleans which ran by electricity. I wondered how the part that ran up to the power line over head stayed on the large wire. I never rode one that I remember. I also saw them in San Francisco.

The lady also reminded me of the small cars that ran off of a battery. It was made a little different than a golf cart, but as I remember it was about the size of a golf cart and it had to be put on a charger each night. I only saw one and Uncle Mark Hodges had it. It was streetwise and Mark had someone else drive him around in it. That was one of the things that didn't catch on. It just wasn't fast enough to follow an automobile, and a person couldn't see too well around it or over it either.

A neighbor lady told me that in her family there were three girls. She and another one of the three would walk down the street they lived on and tried to find a penny so they could buy some candy. For a penny they could buy two pieces, one for each of them. They felt a lot of joy from their find.

Mr. Walker, a neighbor that lived on our street in the 1950s and 1960s, told me of living in Houston in the hard days with his wife. He said they needed a house so they found an empty one and they moved in. When the owner found that they were living in his house, he ran them out. So they looked for another empty one. When they discovered another one, they moved in until they were found as before. It became routine for them to move a lot until jobs begin to open up.

James Ray, Uncle James' oldest child, came to our house one day. He lived in the city and we, or it could have been just me, wished we could live in the city, so we wouldn't have chores, field work and all the other work to do and thought we would have plenty of fun when school shut down for the summer. I didn't think we country kids were maybe the ones that had the most fun when work was all caught up. We had all that land to roam in. The woods and good fishing places were so much better than the streets of Hattiesburg.

Anyway, James Ray told J.P. and me about a new game. Well, to us it was new. As I remember, it was called cricket. James Ray showed us how long and how big a stick needed to be to play cricket. We got a tin can as a ball, and there was a line to be drawn through the grass for the goal. Now we were ready to play. We put the can between the goals like basketball. I think we tapped the ground, tapped each other's stick so many times, and started swinging and see who could get the can to our goal first.

Where did he get the sticks to play with? I don't know, but Uncle James ran a glass and hardware store for a man. He must have either gotten them from out of the city or pieces of lumber from the store.

Bill Brown's house which still stands.

193

Culture Change

Our culture has changed so much. We use to have plenty of room here in the USA with farms where poor people used to live. Now the poor people have gone to the city to find work to live. We live so close to the neighbors, a man and his wife go to bed at night and have to be real quiet. At the time of the evening stillness, it is time to forget about the everyday grind. Time to just lie back and relax and enjoy the night together and try to forget about the alarm clock going off, until it does that is. Don't forget about the neighbors now, and don't get too loud because gossip runs like water. The more we talk out loud, the more it runs from family to family until everyone knows your business.

On the farm, we could be gone for several days and no one would miss us unless someone came by for a little companionship for awhile or needed to borrow something, except who ever we asked to come by each day to do chores. That wasn't very often since we didn't have money to go very far. Now, we have jobs, we can take holidays and vacation time off with pay, and be able to see how other people live. We even have insurance to help pay a visit to the doctor sometimes.

We used to walk to church or the grocery store which was about three miles away. Now we drive to go to church or the grocery store and park as close as possible to the door so we will not have so far to walk.

Men would leave their homes to go on jobs, if they were lucky and had money-making jobs, and also do work on the farm. The women also worked on the farm and did women's work such as wash clothes, iron, keep eyes on kids to help get them raised. Now, our culture has both Mama and Daddy working away from home while we pay someone else to come in and raise the kids so we can make a living. The kids probably wonder "Who is the real mother?", but it now takes both to make enough money to keep up and pay bills.

We cooked and warmed by a fire made by good wood, and we had plenty of wood to cut and burn. The people who lived on the prairies of West Texas, Oklahoma, and other places that were treeless had to use things like cow chips they could get from the pastures, open land or wherever the cows were. Chips? No, that isn't what cow chips are. Not just a slice off the cow, but what falls from the cow to the ground and lays there until it gets rotted enough for the grass to eat it. Then the cow and the grass are happy. Then the cow eats the grass and the cycle starts over again.

We could hold a cow around the neck with our head up against the cow and it felt so good. Who can love up to a hot lawn mower these days? We have gone from dusty roads to concrete freeways, from walking to riding.

Early one morning on my way to work, I came to a freeway that led to my place of work and turned down the feeder road to enter the freeway. Before I got on it, I saw blinking lights up ahead on the feeder road. Some of the lights were up a little high and others down low. I thought maybe I wanted to do some rubber necking, so I stayed on the feeder road to get a good look at what the problem was. After passing the ramp, I saw the lights were on a garbage truck. As a kid, if someone had a heart attack or maybe appendicitis, that was something to get excited about, but what is so exciting about a city garbage truck?

With no refrigerator to keep milk from getting sour, it would be called blue-john. It sure made good biscuits, but was not good to drink. We could wait awhile though, and when it clabbered up it was good again. City milk doesn't work that way when it is pasteurized.

When I was young, I thought people that had a slop jar had a lot of money. We had to go out in the yard at night when nature called because we didn't have a slop jar in cold weather, rain or whatever. When people started buying well pumps to bring water from the wells into the houses, people also started building the toilets inside the houses. I thought about that entire stench that would go along with it and didn't know how to accept that. I was talking to Roland Travis about the outhouse going into the house. He said he didn't think he wanted an outhouse inside his house either and have to put up with that stench that comes with it. I knew I had a friend that thought the same way I did. Sitting at the table eating and the stench lazily drifting through the dining room would be hard to accept.

When a man had a car, and the car stopped for some reason, he would step out of it and wait. A car would come by, and there wasn't any way to know when, but when it did, usually the man would be helped even if it was only to hitch a ride to town. Now, if I plan to have car trouble on the road, I best put a little money in my pocket.

Revisiting The Old Eddy with Marvin Carpenter's second wife, Lucy Ree Clark Carpenter and Lee Alan Travis.

Precious Memories

I saw things in those woods on our way to and from the Old Eddy that are no longer there. Things had changed so much in my lifetime. The earth, I guess, is in a constant change like people. I saw how the trees changed, leaving a good passage beneath them to losing ground or being cut down or dying. The brush would take over and fight to grow up, causing thick growth and hard areas to walk through. In my mind I saw where fields had been and the forests the fields came from are back again. It made me think of the Indians being in the swamps. I was told how Indians lived on the hills on one side of us, where they made arrows and went down into Tallahala swamps to hunt. That made me think about the people changing. The Indians stunk, I was told, and some liked to dress up their hair with blood and cow dung. Their lifestyle may have given them a bad aroma. When men kissed their ladies that might have made their breath stink.

Before I was born the timber had never been cut over, making me think how beautiful the landscape must have been. It is sad to think how people change the earth. The

Indians were first to be here and they let white men come in. Then "being nice" was the same as being destroyed by the people. They were nice too. J.P. read the book, <u>The Trail of Tears</u>, and said he had always felt sorry for the black slaves until then. The white men wanted the blacks to live and do their work, but wanted the Indians to die. I wonder if when I die I may see my older generation people from years ago and recognize them. I would like to, especially the pretty ladies.

The arrowheads must've been made from rock from the river. The Indians may have put them in sacks on the backs of horses and carried them down the hills. I am sure sacks would have been made of cowhide, buffalo hide, or hide from any dead animal. I am sure that they didn't make sacks from live animals.

While there, it seemed as though everything was sleeping. No wind. The air wasn't moving anything. Only we people moved around. The earth, water, and trees seemed to be lonely. Sleeping or just resting. Nothing saying, "I'm moving on." I didn't want to leave from there, but reality had a pull on me. We had to go. Looking behind, the land had different generations, different people, and different culture. That would change anything.

I stood looking at the scenery. Out in the roadway, it was too thick with bushes to see only a few feet or a few yards away. I remembered enjoying myself, sitting on the ground on the roots of a large tree with my back resting against the body of the tree, looking out many yards in some direction, being very quiet, letting my mind wonder around while my eyes were doing the same thing, listening to the quietness except for an animal or bird playing around or running through the leaves and at the same time keeping an eye on me to be sure I wasn't a threat to them. I would sit there just drinking all that in. Take a break from reality and enjoy God's gift to his people and wonder if God himself was enjoying what He was seeing; the sounds occasionally coming from the barking of a squirrel taking notice on me, the calling of a crow, or the singing of a bird. At the time I thought I would always have that kind of atmosphere and sort of took it all for granted, not knowing how much I was enjoying all of that. It seemed that sometimes we get away from the good, and we can see the things of our past much more clearly with our eyes shut and our minds open to the memory of our past. Life was hard back then, but memories are rich today because of our good times with good things and good people of our past.

Carpenter with his great grandson, Levi Robinson (who inherited Marvin's love of nature and fishing!)

In Closing

Well, as some would say back in the old days, "Well, I have told you my story and we have had fun, but now I will let you go. I now have places to go, and things to do, so I better light a shuck and run."

I hope that you will remember part of what I have said about myself, back when I was a young sprout. If I see you before you see me, I will holler.

Let's Go Fishing

JP and I,
When we were small
Did things together;
Work, play and all.

We found excitement
Wherever we'd go
Sometimes fishing
A few hours or so

Only when there was
No work to do
Or was not cold
And the sky was blue

When you saw one
You saw the other,
After all,
He was my brother

He dug in dirt
To find a worm.
When he got tired
It was my turn.

Crawfish came second
To our command.
We caught a bunch

All by hand.

Off with the hooks
And line in hand
We ran the trail
Over dirt and sand.

Through fields and woods
We would quickly go
Down by the neighbors
And down the fence row.

Sometimes we would talk
And make our plan.
We'd run through briars
Bushes and land.

We stayed together,
Him and me,
Who'd catch the most fish?
We shall see.

Down to the Eddy
We would go,
It was may be
A mile or so.

That old Eddy
Was deep and wide
Lot of moss
For the fish to hide.

When we'd go there

Marvin Carpenter

We'd cut a pole
To reach way out
In that hole

We'd string up bait
Then take a look
For the very best place
To set a hook

In the edge of the water
We would stand
Being quiet and still
As we can

Fish would hang up
Sometimes on the moss
He would get off
But that's no loss

When the fish grew
He'd be back
He'd find himself
In our sack

We would fish on
And do our best
To catch enough fish
To have a mess

We strung our fish
On a forked stick
After getting a bite
And we were quick

We stuck our fish
Under the moss
They didn't live long
Their lives were lost

The sun got hot
Our chances slim
Off came our clothes
For a little swim

When we got through
We'd check our fish
For them to be turned up
Wasn't our wish

We'd take them home
Through the sand and heat
They'd yellow up
Looking quite beat

When we got home
And Mama saw us
We didn't have many fish
But she didn't make any fuss!

Riding The Raft

Ralph and I, we had a plan.
We would build a raft, and sail the river.
We knew for sure, we were good.
I learned later, some memories are forever.

We went to the swamp, looked around
To see what we could use.
Lots of logs, but they'd soak up water.
Then saw a dead tree, we just couldn't lose.

Down the river, we would go
It'd hold us both, we're sure
Couldn't wait, to carry out our plan
Had traveling fever, but there's a cure

We found a tree, tall and dry
Just the one, that looked the best
We'd cut it down, sawed it up
Then we could take a rest

We would sail, down the river
Enjoy the ride, and see the scene
What we didn't know, about a raft
That old river, could be mean

We left and went home with our plan
And had to wait a few days
Till we had plenty of time, to do our stuff

Before that old tree decays

We got the hammer, and saw from the garage
Broken pickets, from the fence
Our nails from under, the old wash pot
And down the road we went

About a mile, we had to go
With nails, tools and wood
Would we get tired, before we arrive?
We knew we surely would

We sat down, got us some rest
Then was on our way
We had plenty of work to do
We had been waiting for that day

We got there threw down our stuff
The old tree was still standing there
Waiting for us to cut it down
The old tree and us had a trip to share

We got all ready, and began to saw
And when it came tearing down
As it fell through the other trees
Our tree made a terrible sound

We had it down and took a look
Where would we cut it first?
Just how long shall we cut the thing?
Too long, too short, which is worse?

We cut each piece about six feet

I think that's what there were
As long as we had room to stand
We didn't worry we really didn't care

A raft that size is too large
To take it all at one time
We took each log, one by one
Right on down to the water line

When we got them to the water
Putting them all side by side
Now we can start to nail them down
With broken pickets till we're satisfied

We hoped the nails from beneath the wash pot
Will not come loose, and let us down
Seems they should have gone much deeper
We hope they don't start breaking down

We made the raft close to the stream
So we could move it, all about
When we got ready, to make a go
We could move it right on out.

We put the raft between some logs
That had fallen into the stream
They had settled, deep in the sand
Anchored down very good it seems

With the raft pulled into the shallows
Looked as if it was safe to leave
Unless rain came, to bring a flood
Then it'd be headed for the seas

We went on back to the house
To wait for another day
If the river rise and the raft is gone
Ralph and I will have to pay

Anxiety was getting the best of me
I just couldn't wait, for our day
We had a lot of work and chores to do
Mama was the one that was to say

When our day came, and we had time
We were off to the river swamp
We're about to find when we get there
There's lots of work that we don't want

When we got back, to the river swamp
Everything looked just as it should
But the water dropped low and the raft was high
Will the thing float? We'll see if it would

We had found a paddle, down in some drift
We shall need that, most of all
But when we tried to pry it loose
It was like pushing on a wall

We needed a pole, to push it around
To get it away, from the log
Without axe or saw, a pole is hard to find
We need the raft out of a bog

We finally found a stick not what we want
But we worked together like a team

Pushing and turning it soon turned loose.
Then floated out into the stream.

Ralph grabbed the paddle, and we jumped aboard
Don't need to be left behind
The thing hit the flow of the swift water
Started turning around now we're in a bind

Ralph took the paddle, to straighten us out
We had never been riding a raft
We didn't know the front from the back
We realized now that the front is the AFT

On that thing there's no fan-tail
What's more there's not even a bow
We began to wonder how that thing could float
Even now, I'm beginning to wonder how

We could see a stump a coming
I mean it was a coming very fast
Those nails would squall but the pickets hung on
We wondered how long they would last

Back then, there were logs in the current
I would think most are still there
They stood high enough; we couldn't miss 'em
I guess they were reaching for air

When we saw danger, up ahead
We rowed hard to reach the sand
One paddled hard as we could
The other was watching where we would land

I know we could've enjoyed that ride
Saw places we'd never seen
If all had of been running real good
But the raft was a acting mean

We found that the current has its way
Nothing we did really worked well
We fought hard trying to stay on
Nothing changed as we could tell

We hit a stump the raft was awash
The water went across our bow
It wasn't time to scuttle that thing
That was all we had right now

We couldn't get to the sand bar
So we could get off of that thing
We were not lucky with the logs and stumps
We hit them all the same

Stumps stuck up from the bottom
Where they had a very good hold
When the old stumps and we came together
We were the ones that felt the jolt

We tried to paddle make the raft go straight
But the thing turned round and round
Something's wrong we can't right the raft
We can't even go around

The current was like a scared mule
With someone on his back
The way it spent us from log to log

A little confidence is what we lack

We ran into a bluff over on the far side
But it was a long way around
Yet we realized that may be ok
As long as our feet were on the ground

We tried to catch on to the bluff
But hand holds were not there
We knew if we didn't catch it now
Our chances would sure be rare

We missed our chances to catch the bluff
Where is the next place to try?
If we get to the mouth of the river
We can kiss a joy ride good bye

Going fishing with a line and pole
On Tallahala is a good place to be
But riding a raft with a strong current
May as well be out at sea

When we came to a curve in the river
It seemed that the water speeded up
I now think it all ran the same
It didn't matter we still needed luck

Thinking as I grew up and learn to swim
I'll have a chance to change my mind
Being scared to death isn't so good
After this it'll take some time

Mom and dad don't know where we are

Things start flashing on my mind
If we don't show up to do the chores
They wouldn't let us go back for a time

Finally we came to a bluff on the river
Where the water went gushing by
A limb from a bush, stuck out our way
I had to get hold on the first try

Ralph grabbed the paddle rowing very hard
Then the raft swung into the bank
We tried to jump both at once
Trying not to fall and sink

We let the raft go down the river
Not ever knowing where it went
We had memories to last for a while
I think now is the time for us to repent

It was a good feeling to be released
From the waters that treated us bad
I'll never forget the way we were treated
One of the worst memories I've ever had

It's been years since Ralph has been gone
And now I'm hot on his trail
Now I think if it all works out
We'll have lots of stories to tell